CompTIA Cloud+ (Plus) Certification

Practice Questions, Answers and Master the Exam

Table of Contents

Introduction

In the ever-evolving landscape of technology, the realm of cloud computing stands as a towering force, reshaping the way businesses operate and revolutionizing the way data is managed. As organizations increasingly migrate their infrastructure to the cloud, the demand for skilled professionals who can navigate this intricate domain has never been higher. CompTIA Cloud+ (Plus) certification emerges as a beacon in this dynamic environment, validating the expertise of individuals in deploying, managing, and securing cloud infrastructure.

This book serves as a comprehensive guide to mastering the CompTIA Cloud+ certification, offering a rich tapestry of practice test questions, detailed answers, and invaluable insights to empower you on your journey to success. Delving into the intricacies of cloud computing, the content within these pages transcends mere exam preparation; it acts as a companion, equipping you with the knowledge and confidence needed to excel in real-world scenarios.

Embark on your Cloud+ certification journey by unraveling the fundamental concepts that underpin cloud computing. From essential terminology to the core principles governing cloud architectures, this section lays the groundwork for a robust understanding of the subject matter. Dive deep into cloud service models, deployment models, and the intricate relationships between them, paving the way for a solid foundation that will be crucial throughout your certification pursuit.

Navigate the complexities of cloud infrastructure with ease as you explore virtualization technologies, storage options, and network configurations. The Cloud+ certification demands a nuanced understanding of how these components seamlessly integrate to form a cohesive and scalable environment. This section provides not only the theoretical knowledge required but also practical insights into implementing and managing cloud infrastructure effectively.

As the cloud becomes an integral part of organizational operations, ensuring the security of data and applications becomes paramount. Arm yourself with the knowledge to identify and mitigate security risks, implement encryption, and fortify access controls. The practice questions and detailed answers in this section simulate real-world scenarios, preparing you to be a vigilant guardian of cloud security in any professional setting.

Elevate your capabilities by delving into the deployment and management of cloud services. From selecting appropriate service models to optimizing resource allocation, this segment equips you with the skills needed to orchestrate seamless cloud operations. Real-world scenarios and practical exercises enhance your proficiency, ensuring you are not just prepared for the exam but also for the challenges of the dynamic cloud landscape.

Even in the cloud, challenges and hiccups are inevitable. Uncover the art of troubleshooting in cloud environments, learning to identify and resolve issues efficiently. Explore optimization techniques to enhance performance and resource utilization, transforming you into a cloud professional capable of not just managing but optimizing cloud infrastructure for peak efficiency.

A key highlight of this book is the extensive collection of practice test questions meticulously crafted to mirror the structure and difficulty of the CompTIA Cloud+ exam. Test your knowledge across various domains, from cloud concepts to security protocols, and receive detailed explanations for each question to solidify your understanding. This hands-on approach not only gauges your readiness for the exam but also fortifies your grasp on the practical aspects of cloud computing.

As you approach the final leg of your preparation, discover effective strategies for acing the CompTIA Cloud+ exam. From time management tips to tackling different question formats, this section serves as a strategic guide to enhance your exam-taking skills. Coupled with the comprehensive content throughout the book, these strategies empower you to confidently face the certification challenge and emerge victorious.

The journey doesn't end with the last page of this book—it culminates in the attainment of the CompTIA Cloud+ certification. Unveil the significance of this achievement in the professional landscape and open doors to a myriad of opportunities in cloud computing. Whether you are aiming to advance your current career or embark on a new path, the Cloud+ certification is a testament to your expertise and commitment to excellence in the ever-expanding world of cloud technology.

In your hands, you hold more than a preparation guide; you possess a comprehensive companion that empowers you to not only pass the CompTIA Cloud+ exam but also to excel in the dynamic and challenging domain of cloud computing. Let the journey begin, and may the cloud be ever in your favor.

Chapter 1: Introducing Cloud Computing Configurations and Deployments

Introducing Cloud Computing

Cloud computing, at its core, revolutionizes the traditional approach to IT infrastructure. It is not merely a technological shift; it represents a paradigm change in the way organizations leverage resources, deliver services, and manage data.

Defining Cloud Computing:

Cloud computing is a model for delivering on-demand computing resources over the internet. Understanding its three fundamental service models—Infrastructure as a Service (IaaS), Platform as a Service (PaaS), and Software as a Service (SaaS)—provides a comprehensive insight into the diverse offerings within the cloud ecosystem.

Key Characteristics of Cloud Computing:

Examine the five essential characteristics—on-demand self-service, broad network access, resource pooling, rapid elasticity, and measured service—that distinguish cloud computing from traditional models. Each characteristic contributes to the agility, scalability, and efficiency that define the cloud.

Advantages of Cloud Computing:

Uncover the tangible benefits that drive organizations to adopt cloud solutions, such as cost savings, flexibility, and the ability to focus on core business functions. Explore real-world examples illustrating how cloud computing transforms operational landscapes, making it a strategic asset for businesses of all sizes.

Creating and Validating a Cloud Deployment

Creating a robust cloud deployment involves meticulous planning, precise execution, and continuous validation to ensure optimal performance.

Planning a Cloud Deployment:

Before delving into the technical aspects, grasp the significance of strategic planning. Understand how to assess organizational needs, select appropriate service models, and define deployment goals. Effective planning lays the foundation for a successful cloud journey.

Selecting Cloud Deployment Models:

Explore the various deployment models—public, private, hybrid, and community—and comprehend the factors influencing their selection. This section provides a detailed comparison, enabling you to make informed decisions based on security, control, and scalability requirements.

Executing a Cloud Deployment:

Navigate the deployment process, from provisioning resources to configuring services. Understand the role of orchestration and automation in streamlining deployment tasks, ensuring consistency and efficiency. Real-world examples illuminate best practices for a seamless deployment experience.

Verifying System Requirements

Verification of system requirements is a critical aspect of maintaining a stable and secure cloud infrastructure. In this section, delve into the meticulous process of validating system prerequisites to guarantee the compatibility and performance of your cloud deployment.

Hardware and Software Compatibility:

Uncover the importance of ensuring that hardware components and software applications meet the specified compatibility criteria. Learn how to conduct thorough assessments to prevent compatibility issues that could impede the functionality of your cloud environment.

Network Infrastructure Validation:

Explore the intricacies of validating network components, including bandwidth, latency, and security protocols. Understand how a well-optimized network infrastructure contributes to the overall performance and responsiveness of cloud-based applications and services.

Security and Compliance Checks:

Delve into the world of security validation, encompassing identity management, access controls, and compliance requirements. Learn to conduct rigorous security audits to identify vulnerabilities and ensure that your cloud deployment adheres to industry standards and regulatory frameworks.

Practice Questions and Answers

Question 1:

What is the primary characteristic that distinguishes cloud computing from traditional models?

A. Broad Network Access

B. Rapid Elasticity

C. On-Demand Self-Service

D. Resource Pooling

Answer: B - Rapid Elasticity

Explanation: Rapid elasticity is a key characteristic of cloud computing that allows resources to scale up or down quickly based on demand. While the other options (A, C, D) are also characteristics of cloud computing, rapid elasticity specifically addresses the dynamic scalability aspect.

Question 2:

Which service model involves providing users with access to virtualized computing resources over the internet?

A. Infrastructure as a Service (IaaS)

B. Platform as a Service (PaaS)

C. Software as a Service (SaaS)

D. Hybrid as a Service (HaaS)

Answer: A - Infrastructure as a Service (IaaS)

Explanation: IaaS delivers virtualized computing resources over the internet, allowing users to manage and control the underlying infrastructure. PaaS and SaaS provide higher-level services, and HaaS is not a recognized cloud service model.

Question 3:

What is a characteristic of a public cloud deployment model?

A. Shared Resources

B. Limited Accessibility

C. Exclusive Ownership

D. Isolated Environment

Answer: A - Shared Resources

Explanation: Public clouds involve shared resources, making infrastructure and services available to the general public. Private clouds (options B, C, D) typically have limited accessibility, exclusive ownership, and an isolated environment.

Question 4:

In the context of cloud computing, what is the role of orchestration?

A. Resource Provisioning

B. Infrastructure Security

C. Network Configuration

D. Service Monitoring

Answer: A - Resource Provisioning

Explanation: Orchestration in cloud computing involves automating and coordinating tasks to provision and manage resources efficiently. While options B, C, and D are essential aspects of cloud computing, orchestration specifically addresses resource provisioning.

Question 5:

What is the primary goal of validating system requirements in a cloud deployment?

A. Enhancing Performance

B. Ensuring Compatibility

C. Improving Security

D. Streamlining Orchestration

Answer: B - Ensuring Compatibility

Explanation: Validating system requirements ensures that hardware, software, and network components are compatible, reducing the risk of deployment issues. While performance, security, and orchestration are important, ensuring compatibility is the primary goal during validation.

Question 6:

Which deployment model involves the use of both on-premises infrastructure and public cloud services?

A. Public Cloud

B. Private Cloud

C. Hybrid Cloud

D. Community Cloud

Answer: C - Hybrid Cloud

Explanation: Hybrid cloud deployment combines on-premises infrastructure with public cloud services. Public, private, and community clouds (options A, B, D) have distinct characteristics and deployment models.

Question 7:

What does "measured service" refer to in cloud computing?

A. Pay-per-Use

B. Unlimited Access

C. Dedicated Resources

D. Exclusive Contracts

Answer: A - Pay-per-Use

Explanation: Measured service in cloud computing refers to the pay-per-use model, where users are billed based on their usage. Options B, C, and D do not specifically relate to the concept of measured service.

Question 8:

Which component is crucial for ensuring the security of a cloud deployment?

A. Load Balancer

B. Firewall

C. Router

D. Switch

Answer: B - Firewall

Explanation: Firewalls play a vital role in securing a cloud deployment by controlling and monitoring incoming and outgoing network traffic. While options A, C, and D are network components, a firewall is specifically designed for security purposes.

Question 9:

What is the primary benefit of using Platform as a Service (PaaS)?

A. Infrastructure Management

B. Application Development

C. Network Configuration

D. Virtualization Control

Answer: B - Application Development

Explanation: PaaS provides a platform for developers to build, deploy, and manage applications without dealing with the underlying infrastructure. While IaaS (option A) focuses on infrastructure management, PaaS is specifically geared towards application development.

Question 10:

In a private cloud deployment, what is a defining characteristic?

A. Shared Resources

B. Limited Accessibility

C. Exclusive Ownership

D. Public Accessibility

Answer: C - Exclusive Ownership

Explanation: Private clouds are dedicated to a single organization, offering exclusive ownership and control over the infrastructure. Shared resources, limited accessibility, and public accessibility (options A, B, D) are characteristic of other deployment models.

Question 11:

Which characteristic allows cloud users to access services from anywhere over the internet?

A. On-Demand Self-Service

B. Broad Network Access

C. Resource Pooling

D. Rapid Elasticity

Answer: B - Broad Network Access

Explanation: Broad network access enables cloud services to be accessed from various devices and locations over the internet. On-demand self-service, resource pooling, and rapid elasticity (options A, C, D) are other essential characteristics but do not specifically address accessibility.

Question 12:

What is the purpose of resource pooling in cloud computing?

A. Ensuring Compatibility

B. Improving Security

C. Efficient Resource Utilization

D. Streamlining Orchestration

Answer: C - Efficient Resource Utilization

Explanation: Resource pooling involves aggregating resources to serve multiple users, promoting efficient utilization. While compatibility, security, and orchestration (options A, B, D) are important, resource pooling focuses on optimization.

Question 13:

Which cloud service model allows users to consume applications without managing the underlying infrastructure?

A. Infrastructure as a Service (IaaS)

B. Platform as a Service (PaaS)

C. Software as a Service (SaaS)

D. Function as a Service (FaaS)

Answer: C - Software as a Service (SaaS)

Explanation: SaaS allows users to consume applications without managing the underlying infrastructure. IaaS, PaaS, and FaaS (options A, B, D) provide different levels of service and control.

Question 14:

What term is used to describe the dynamic allocation and deallocation of computing resources in response to demand?

A. Elastic Computing

B. Virtualization

C. Load Balancing

D. Clustering

Answer: A - Elastic Computing

Explanation: Elastic computing refers to the dynamic scaling of resources in response to changing demand. Virtualization, load balancing, and clustering (options B, C, D) are related concepts but do not specifically address dynamic resource allocation.

Question 15:

Which deployment model is characterized by a cloud infrastructure shared by several organizations with common interests?

A. Public Cloud

B. Private Cloud

C. Hybrid Cloud

D. Community Cloud

Answer: D - Community Cloud

Explanation: Community clouds are shared by organizations with common interests, providing a collaborative and secure cloud infrastructure. Public, private, and hybrid clouds (options A, B, C) have different characteristics and use cases.

Question 16:

What is the primary goal of on-demand self-service in cloud computing?

A. Ensuring Compatibility

B. Improving Security

C. Streamlining Orchestration

D. Enabling User Autonomy

Answer: D - Enabling User Autonomy

Explanation: On-demand self-service allows users to provision and manage resources independently, promoting user autonomy. Compatibility, security, and orchestration (options A, B, C) are important but do not directly address user autonomy.

Question 17:

Which cloud deployment model offers the highest level of control and customization?

A. Public Cloud

B. Private Cloud

C. Hybrid Cloud

D. Community Cloud

Answer: B - Private Cloud

Explanation: Private clouds provide exclusive ownership and control, offering the highest level of customization and control. Public, hybrid, and community clouds (options A, C, D) have varying levels of control and shared resources.

Question 18:

What is the primary advantage of using measured service in cloud computing?

A. Predictable Costs

B. Unlimited Access

C. Dedicated Resources

D. Exclusive Contracts

Answer: A - Predictable Costs

Explanation: Measured service allows users to be billed based on actual usage, providing predictable and cost-effective pricing. Options B, C, and D do not specifically address the advantage of predictable costs.

Question 19:

Which cloud computing characteristic refers to the ability to rapidly scale resources up or down based on demand?

A. On-Demand Self-Service

B. Broad Network Access

C. Resource Pooling

D. Rapid Elasticity

Answer: D - Rapid Elasticity

Explanation: Rapid elasticity enables dynamic scaling of resources to meet changing demand, ensuring flexibility and efficiency. On-demand self-service, broad network access, and resource pooling (options A, B, C) are other essential characteristics.

Question 20:

In cloud computing, what is the primary purpose of network configuration?

A. Resource Provisioning

B. Infrastructure Security

C. Application Development

D. Load Balancing

Answer: B - Infrastructure Security

Explanation: Network configuration in cloud computing primarily focuses on securing the infrastructure by implementing protocols, firewalls, and access controls. Resource provisioning, application development, and load balancing (options A, C, D) are related but have different purposes.

Question 21:

What deployment model provides a combination of on-premises infrastructure and dedicated cloud resources for a single organization?

A. Public Cloud

B. Private Cloud

C. Hybrid Cloud

D. Community Cloud

Answer: C - Hybrid Cloud

Explanation: Hybrid clouds combine on-premises infrastructure with dedicated cloud resources, offering a flexible and scalable solution. Public, private, and community clouds (options A, B, D) have distinct characteristics and use cases.

Question 22:

What characteristic allows cloud users to access services on a pay-as-you-go basis?

A. On-Demand Self-Service

B. Broad Network Access

C. Measured Service

D. Rapid Elasticity

Answer: C - Measured Service

Explanation: Measured service in cloud computing allows users to pay based on actual usage, ensuring a cost-effective pay-as-you-go model. On-demand self-service, broad network access, and rapid elasticity (options A, B, D) are other important characteristics.

Question 23:

Which deployment model is suitable for organizations with specific security and compliance requirements?

A. Public Cloud

B. Private Cloud

C. Hybrid Cloud

D. Community Cloud

Answer: B - Private Cloud

Explanation: Private clouds are dedicated to a single organization, providing exclusive control and meeting specific security and compliance requirements. Public, hybrid, and community clouds (options A, C, D) have different characteristics and use cases.

Question 24:

What is the primary goal of network validation in a cloud deployment?

A. Ensuring Compatibility

B. Improving Security

C. Efficient Resource Utilization

D. Verifying Performance

Answer: B - Improving Security

Explanation: Network validation in a cloud deployment focuses on ensuring security by verifying components like firewalls, access controls, and encryption protocols. Compatibility, efficient resource utilization, and performance (options A, C, D) are important but do not directly address security.

Question 25:

Which cloud service model is focused on providing a runtime environment for executing code in response to events?

A. Infrastructure as a Service (IaaS)

B. Platform as a Service (PaaS)

C. Software as a Service (SaaS)

D. Function as a Service (FaaS)

Answer: D - Function as a Service (FaaS)

Explanation: FaaS provides a runtime environment for executing code in response to events, allowing developers to focus on specific functions. IaaS, PaaS, and SaaS (options A, B, C) offer different levels of service and control.

Question 26:

Which deployment model involves multiple organizations sharing cloud resources based on common concerns, such as security or compliance?

A. Public Cloud

B. Private Cloud

C. Hybrid Cloud

D. Community Cloud

Answer: D - Community Cloud

Explanation: Community clouds involve multiple organizations sharing resources based on common concerns, fostering collaboration and addressing shared security or compliance requirements. Public, private, and hybrid clouds (options A, B, C) have different characteristics.

Question 27:

What is the primary role of a load balancer in cloud computing?

A. Ensuring Compatibility

B. Improving Security

C. Efficient Resource Utilization

D. Distributing Workload

Answer: D - Distributing Workload

Explanation: Load balancers distribute incoming network traffic across multiple servers, ensuring efficient resource utilization and preventing overload on any single server. Compatibility, security, and resource utilization (options A, B, C) are important but do not directly address workload distribution.

Question 28:

What characteristic allows cloud users to provision computing resources as needed without human intervention?

A. On-Demand Self-Service

B. Broad Network Access

C. Rapid Elasticity

D. Measured Service

Answer: A - On-Demand Self-Service

Explanation: On-demand self-service in cloud computing allows users to provision and manage resources without human intervention, promoting autonomy. Broad network access, rapid elasticity, and measured service (options B, C, D) are other essential characteristics.

Question 29:

Which characteristic allows cloud users to adjust resources automatically based on workload fluctuations?

A. On-Demand Self-Service

B. Broad Network Access

C. Rapid Elasticity

D. Measured Service

Answer: C - Rapid Elasticity

Explanation: Rapid elasticity allows cloud resources to automatically scale up or down based on workload fluctuations, ensuring flexibility and efficiency. On-demand self-service, broad network access, and measured service (options A, B, D) are other essential characteristics.

Question 30:

What is the primary advantage of using measured service in cloud computing?

A. Predictable Costs

B. Unlimited Access

C. Dedicated Resources

D. Exclusive Contracts

Answer: A - Predictable Costs

Explanation: Measured service allows users to be billed based on actual usage, providing predictable and cost-effective pricing. Options B, C, and D do not specifically address the advantage of predictable costs.

Question 31:

Which characteristic allows cloud users to access services on a pay-as-you-go basis?

A. On-Demand Self-Service

B. Broad Network Access

C. Measured Service

D. Rapid Elasticity

Answer: C - Measured Service

Explanation: Measured service in cloud computing allows users to pay based on actual usage, ensuring a cost-effective pay-as-you-go model. On-demand self-service, broad network access, and rapid elasticity (options A, B, D) are other important characteristics.

Question 32:

What deployment model is characterized by a cloud infrastructure shared by several organizations with common interests?

A. Public Cloud

B. Private Cloud

C. Hybrid Cloud

D. Community Cloud

Answer: D - Community Cloud

Explanation: Community clouds are shared by organizations with common interests, providing a collaborative and secure cloud infrastructure. Public, private, and hybrid clouds (options A, B, C) have distinct characteristics and use cases.

Question 33:

What characteristic allows cloud users to access services from anywhere over the internet?

A. On-Demand Self-Service

B. Broad Network Access

C. Resource Pooling

D. Rapid Elasticity

Answer: B - Broad Network Access

Explanation: Broad network access enables cloud services to be accessed from various devices and locations over the internet. On-demand self-service, resource pooling, and rapid elasticity (options A, C, D) are other essential characteristics but do not specifically address accessibility.

Question 34:

Which deployment model offers the highest level of control and customization?

A. Public Cloud

B. Private Cloud

C. Hybrid Cloud

D. Community Cloud

Answer: B - Private Cloud

Explanation: Private clouds provide exclusive ownership and control, offering the highest level of customization and control. Public, hybrid, and community clouds (options A, C, D) have varying levels of control and shared resources.

Question 35:

In cloud computing, what is the primary purpose of network configuration?

A. Resource Provisioning

B. Infrastructure Security

C. Application Development

D. Load Balancing

Answer: B - Infrastructure Security

Explanation: Network configuration in cloud computing primarily focuses on securing the infrastructure by implementing protocols, firewalls, and access controls. Resource provisioning, application development, and load balancing (options A, C, D) are related but have different purposes.

Question 36:

What is the primary goal of network validation in a cloud deployment?

A. Ensuring Compatibility

B. Improving Security

C. Efficient Resource Utilization

D. Verifying Performance

Answer: B - Improving Security

Explanation: Network validation in a cloud deployment focuses on ensuring security by verifying components like firewalls, access controls, and encryption protocols. Compatibility, efficient resource utilization, and performance (options A, C, D) are important but do not directly address security.

Question 37:

Which cloud service model is focused on providing a runtime environment for executing code in response to events?

A. Infrastructure as a Service (IaaS)

B. Platform as a Service (PaaS)

C. Software as a Service (SaaS)

D. Function as a Service (FaaS)

Answer: D - Function as a Service (FaaS)

Explanation: FaaS provides a runtime environment for executing code in response to events, allowing developers to focus on specific functions. IaaS, PaaS, and SaaS (options A, B, C) offer different levels of service and control.

Question 38:

Which deployment model involves multiple organizations sharing cloud resources based on common concerns, such as security or compliance?

A. Public Cloud

B. Private Cloud

C. Hybrid Cloud

D. Community Cloud

Answer: D - Community Cloud

Explanation: Community clouds involve multiple organizations sharing resources based on common concerns, fostering collaboration and addressing shared security or compliance requirements. Public, private, and hybrid clouds (options A, B, C) have different characteristics.

Question 39:

What is the primary role of a load balancer in cloud computing?

A. Ensuring Compatibility

B. Improving Security

C. Efficient Resource Utilization

D. Distributing Workload

Answer: D - Distributing Workload

Explanation: Load balancers distribute incoming network traffic across multiple servers, ensuring efficient resource utilization and preventing overload on any single server. Compatibility, security, and resource utilization (options A, B, C) are important but do not directly address workload distribution.

Question 40:

What characteristic allows cloud users to provision computing resources as needed without human intervention?

A. On-Demand Self-Service

B. Broad Network Access

C. Rapid Elasticity

D. Measured Service

Answer: A - On-Demand Self-Service

Explanation: On-demand self-service in cloud computing allows users to provision and manage resources without human intervention, promoting autonomy. Broad network access, rapid elasticity, and measured service (options B, C, D) are other essential characteristics.

Question 41:

Which characteristic allows cloud users to adjust resources automatically based on workload fluctuations?

A. On-Demand Self-Service

B. Broad Network Access

C. Rapid Elasticity

D. Measured Service

Answer: C - Rapid Elasticity

Explanation: Rapid elasticity allows cloud resources to automatically scale up or down based on workload fluctuations, ensuring flexibility and efficiency. On-demand self-service, broad network access, and measured service (options A, B, D) are other essential characteristics.

Question 42:

What is the primary advantage of using measured service in cloud computing?

A. Predictable Costs

B. Unlimited Access

C. Dedicated Resources

D. Exclusive Contracts

Answer: A - Predictable Costs

Explanation: Measured service allows users to be billed based on actual usage, providing predictable and cost-effective pricing. Options B, C, and D do not specifically address the advantage of predictable costs.

Question 43:

Which characteristic allows cloud users to access services on a pay-as-you-go basis?

A. On-Demand Self-Service

B. Broad Network Access

C. Measured Service

D. Rapid Elasticity

Answer: C - Measured Service

Explanation: Measured service in cloud computing allows users to pay based on actual usage, ensuring a cost-effective pay-as-you-go model. On-demand self-service, broad network access, and rapid elasticity (options A, B, D) are other important characteristics.

Question 44:

What deployment model is characterized by a cloud infrastructure shared by several organizations with common interests?

A. Public Cloud

B. Private Cloud

C. Hybrid Cloud

D. Community Cloud

Answer: D - Community Cloud

Explanation: Community clouds are shared by organizations with common interests, providing a collaborative and secure cloud infrastructure. Public, private, and hybrid clouds (options A, B, C) have distinct characteristics and use cases.

Question 45:

What characteristic allows cloud users to access services from anywhere over the internet?

A. On-Demand Self-Service

B. Broad Network Access

C. Resource Pooling

D. Rapid Elasticity

Answer: B - Broad Network Access

Explanation: Broad network access enables cloud services to be accessed from various devices and locations over the internet. On-demand self-service, resource pooling, and rapid elasticity (options A, C, D) are other essential characteristics but do not specifically address accessibility.

Question 46:

Which deployment model offers the highest level of control and customization?

A. Public Cloud

B. Private Cloud

C. Hybrid Cloud

D. Community Cloud

Answer: B - Private Cloud

Explanation: Private clouds provide exclusive ownership and control, offering the highest level of customization and control. Public, hybrid, and community clouds (options A, C, D) have varying levels of control and shared resources.

Question 47:

In cloud computing, what is the primary purpose of network configuration?

A. Resource Provisioning

B. Infrastructure Security

C. Application Development

D. Load Balancing

Answer: B - Infrastructure Security

Explanation: Network configuration in cloud computing primarily focuses on securing the infrastructure by implementing protocols, firewalls, and access controls. Resource provisioning, application development, and load balancing (options A, C, D) are related but have different purposes.

Question 48:

What is the primary goal of network validation in a cloud deployment?

A. Ensuring Compatibility

B. Improving Security

C. Efficient Resource Utilization

D. Verifying Performance

Answer: B - Improving Security

Explanation: Network validation in a cloud deployment focuses on ensuring security by verifying components like firewalls, access controls, and encryption protocols. Compatibility, efficient resource utilization, and performance (options A, C, D) are important but do not directly address security.

Question 49:

Which cloud service model is focused on providing a runtime environment for executing code in response to events?

A. Infrastructure as a Service (IaaS)

B. Platform as a Service (PaaS)

C. Software as a Service (SaaS)

D. Function as a Service (FaaS)

Answer: D - Function as a Service (FaaS)

Explanation: FaaS provides a runtime environment for executing code in response to events, allowing developers to focus on specific functions. IaaS, PaaS, and SaaS (options A, B, C) offer different levels of service and control.

Question 50:

Which deployment model involves multiple organizations sharing cloud resources based on common concerns, such as security or compliance?

A. Public Cloud

B. Private Cloud

C. Hybrid Cloud

D. Community Cloud

Answer: D - Community Cloud

Explanation: Community clouds involve multiple organizations sharing resources based on common concerns, fostering collaboration and addressing shared security or compliance requirements. Public, private, and hybrid clouds (options A, B, C) have different characteristics.

Chapter 2: Cloud Deployments

Executing a Cloud Deployment

Executing a successful cloud deployment involves a combination of strategic planning, precise implementation, and ongoing management.

Planning and Preparation:

Before diving into the execution phase, understand the importance of meticulous planning and preparation. Explore the key considerations, including workload assessment, resource requirements, and potential challenges. This section provides a roadmap for creating a deployment plan that aligns with organizational goals.

Automation and Orchestration:

Automation and orchestration play a pivotal role in streamlining deployment tasks and ensuring consistency. Learn how to leverage automation tools and orchestration frameworks to accelerate the deployment process while minimizing the risk of human errors. Real-world examples and case studies illustrate the effectiveness of automation in achieving operational efficiency.

Monitoring and Optimization:

Continuous monitoring is crucial for the success of a cloud deployment. Explore the tools and techniques for monitoring key performance indicators, resource utilization, and security metrics. Additionally, understand the importance of ongoing optimization to adapt to changing workloads, control costs, and enhance overall performance.

Matching Data Center Resources to Cloud Resources

Migrating from traditional data center environments to the cloud requires a thoughtful approach to ensure a seamless transition.

Assessment of Existing Resources:

Begin by conducting a comprehensive assessment of existing data center resources. Understand the current infrastructure, application dependencies, and data storage requirements. This assessment serves as the foundation for making informed decisions during the migration process.

Scalability and Elasticity in the Cloud:

Explore how cloud environments offer scalability and elasticity, allowing organizations to dynamically adjust resources based on demand. Understand the benefits of auto-scaling and how it differs from traditional data center scaling methods. Case studies highlight successful examples of organizations achieving optimal scalability in the cloud.

Migration Strategies:

Delve into various migration strategies, including rehosting (lift and shift), re-platforming, and re-architecting. Assess the suitability of each strategy based on specific business needs and constraints. Practical guidance is provided for choosing the most appropriate migration approach for different scenarios.

Cost Considerations:

Understand the cost implications of migrating data center resources to the cloud. Explore cloud pricing models, cost optimization strategies, and tools for estimating and monitoring costs. Real-world examples showcase how organizations effectively manage and control expenses during and after migration.

Configuring and Deploying Storage

Configuring and deploying storage in a cloud environment is a critical aspect of optimizing performance, ensuring data availability, and meeting the storage needs of diverse workloads.

Storage Options in the Cloud:

Explore the array of storage options available in the cloud, including object storage, block storage, and file storage. Understand the characteristics, use cases, and advantages of each storage type. Practical scenarios highlight the suitability of different storage solutions for specific workloads.

Data Backup and Recovery:

Learn the best practices for implementing robust data backup and recovery strategies in the cloud. Explore backup mechanisms, snapshotting, and disaster recovery options. Case studies showcase real-world examples of organizations effectively leveraging cloud storage for data protection.

Scalable Storage Architectures:

Understand how to design scalable storage architectures that can adapt to changing workloads and evolving business requirements. Explore concepts such as sharding, replication, and distributed file systems. Practical guidance is provided for implementing scalable storage solutions that align with organizational growth.

Performing a Server Migration

Server migration is a complex process that requires careful planning and execution to minimize downtime and ensure a smooth transition.

Assessment and Planning:

Begin with a thorough assessment of existing servers, applications, and dependencies. Develop a migration plan that considers factors such as data transfer, application compatibility, and network configurations. Case studies highlight successful server migration projects and the lessons learned.

Migration Tools and Services:

Explore the tools and services available for server migration in the cloud. Understand the capabilities of migration tools provided by cloud service providers and third-party solutions. Practical demonstrations showcase the use of migration tools to streamline the migration process.

Testing and Validation:

Implement testing and validation processes to ensure the integrity and functionality of migrated servers. Explore strategies for conducting pre-migration testing, user acceptance testing, and post-migration validation. Real-world examples illustrate the importance of thorough testing in achieving a successful server migration.

Downtime Mitigation:

Minimize downtime during server migration through strategies such as phased migration, load balancing, and failover configurations. Understand the impact of downtime on business operations and explore techniques for mitigating disruptions. Case studies highlight organizations that successfully executed server migrations with minimal downtime.

Managing User Identities and Roles

Effectively managing user identities and roles is essential for maintaining security, access control, and compliance in a cloud environment.

Identity and Access Management (IAM):

Delve into the concepts of IAM in cloud computing, including user provisioning, access policies, and authentication mechanisms. Understand how to create and manage user identities, groups, and roles. Practical examples demonstrate the implementation of IAM policies for secure access control.

Single Sign-On (SSO) Integration:

Explore the benefits of integrating SSO solutions with cloud platforms to enhance user experience and simplify access management. Understand the integration options available and the impact on security and user workflows. Case studies showcase successful SSO implementations in diverse cloud environments.

Role-Based Access Control (RBAC):

Implement RBAC strategies to assign granular permissions based on user roles and responsibilities. Understand the principles of least privilege and how RBAC enhances security by limiting access to necessary resources. Practical guidance is provided for designing and implementing RBAC models.

Compliance and Auditing:

Explore the role of identity and access management in achieving compliance with regulatory requirements. Understand the importance of audit trails, monitoring, and reporting in demonstrating compliance. Real-world examples illustrate how organizations use IAM tools to meet regulatory standards.

Practice Questions and Answers

Question 1:

What is the primary purpose of meticulous planning in cloud deployment?

A. Enhancing Performance

B. Minimizing Downtime

C. Ensuring Cost Predictability

D. Streamlining Orchestration

Answer: B - Minimizing Downtime

Explanation: Meticulous planning in cloud deployment aims to minimize downtime by identifying potential challenges, creating a deployment plan, and implementing strategies to ensure a smooth transition.

Question 2:

Why is automation important in cloud deployment?

A. To Increase Human Workload

B. To Ensure Manual Control

C. To Streamline Tasks and Ensure Consistency

D. To Introduce Redundancy

Answer: C - To Streamline Tasks and Ensure Consistency

Explanation: Automation in cloud deployment streamlines tasks, reduces human error, and ensures consistency, leading to more efficient and reliable deployments.

Question 3:

What is the primary benefit of continuous monitoring in cloud deployment?

A. Ensuring Compatibility

B. Identifying Performance Issues

C. Minimizing Costs

D. Enhancing Security

Answer: D - Enhancing Security

Explanation: Continuous monitoring in cloud deployment is crucial for enhancing security by identifying and addressing potential threats, vulnerabilities, and suspicious activities.

Question 4:

Which storage type is suitable for unstructured data and scalable workloads, such as media files and backups?

A. Object Storage

B. Block Storage

C. File Storage

D. Cloud Storage

Answer: A - Object Storage

Explanation: Object storage is suitable for unstructured data and scalable workloads, making it ideal for storing media files, backups, and other large datasets.

Question 5:

What is the primary goal of data backup and recovery in cloud storage?

A. Ensuring Data Accessibility

B. Reducing Storage Costs

C. Enhancing Performance

D. Protecting Against Data Loss

Answer: D - Protecting Against Data Loss

Explanation: The primary goal of data backup and recovery in cloud storage is to protect against data loss by creating secure and retrievable copies of critical data.

Question 6:

What is the purpose of scalable storage architectures in cloud deployment?

A. Reducing Security Risks

B. Adapting to Changing Workloads

C. Minimizing Deployment Time

D. Enhancing Network Connectivity

Answer: B - Adapting to Changing Workloads

Explanation: Scalable storage architectures in cloud deployment allow for the adaptation to changing workloads by dynamically adjusting resources based on demand.

Question 7:

Which migration strategy involves moving applications without making any changes, often referred to as a "lift and shift"?

A. Rehosting

B. Re-platforming

C. Re-architecting

D. Refactoring

Answer: A - Rehosting

Explanation: Rehosting, or "lift and shift," involves moving applications to the cloud without making significant changes to their architecture or code.

Question 8:

What is the role of testing and validation in server migration?

A. Ensuring Downtime

B. Identifying Security Vulnerabilities

C. Accelerating Migration

D. Reducing Costs

Answer: B - Identifying Security Vulnerabilities

Explanation: Testing and validation in server migration are essential for identifying security vulnerabilities, ensuring the integrity and functionality of migrated servers.

Question 9:

Why is Single Sign-On (SSO) integration beneficial in managing user identities in the cloud?

A. Increases Complexity

B. Enhances User Experience

C. Decreases Security

D. Requires Multiple Credentials

Answer: B - Enhances User Experience

Explanation: SSO integration in managing user identities enhances user experience by allowing users to access multiple services with a single set of credentials.

Question 10:

What is the primary purpose of Role-Based Access Control (RBAC) in cloud identity management?

A. Increasing Complexity

B. Streamlining Access Management

C. Reducing User Autonomy

D. Minimizing Security

Answer: B - Streamlining Access Management

Explanation: RBAC in cloud identity management streamlines access management by assigning granular permissions based on user roles and responsibilities.

Question 11:

Which cloud storage type is most suitable for databases and virtual machines requiring direct access to block-level storage?

A. Object Storage

B. Block Storage

C. File Storage

D. Cloud Storage

Answer: B - Block Storage

Explanation: Block storage is most suitable for databases and virtual machines requiring direct access to block-level storage for efficient data processing.

Question 12:

What is the primary benefit of using backup mechanisms in cloud storage?

A. Reducing Storage Costs

B. Ensuring Data Accessibility

C. Protecting Against Data Loss

D. Enhancing Performance

Answer: C - Protecting Against Data Loss

Explanation: The primary benefit of using backup mechanisms in cloud storage is protecting against data loss by creating secure and retrievable copies of critical data.

Question 13:

In cloud deployments, what does auto-scaling aim to achieve?

A. Consistency in Performance

B. Static Resource Allocation

C. Dynamic Adjustment of Resources

D. Redundancy in Deployment

Answer: C - Dynamic Adjustment of Resources

Explanation: Auto-scaling in cloud deployments aims to achieve dynamic adjustment of resources based on changing workloads, ensuring optimal performance and resource utilization.

Question 14:

Which migration strategy involves making minimal changes to the application code while optimizing it for the cloud environment?

A. Rehosting

B. Re-platforming

C. Re-architecting

D. Refactoring

Answer: B - Re-platforming

Explanation: Re-platforming involves making minimal changes to the application code while optimizing it for the cloud environment to achieve better performance and efficiency.

Question 15:

What role does load balancing play in server migration to the cloud?

A. Enhancing Security

B. Distributing Workload

C. Reducing Costs

D. Minimizing Downtime

Answer: B - Distributing Workload

Explanation: Load balancing in server migration distributes the workload across multiple servers, ensuring efficient resource utilization and preventing overload on any single server.

Question 16:

Why is identity and access management crucial in achieving regulatory compliance in the cloud?

A. Reducing Security Risks

B. Enhancing User Autonomy

C. Ensuring Data Accessibility

D. Meeting Regulatory Requirements

Answer: D - Meeting Regulatory Requirements

Explanation: Identity and access management in the cloud are crucial for meeting regulatory requirements by ensuring secure access, audit trails, and compliance with specific standards.

Question 17:

What is the primary goal of conducting pre-migration testing in server migration?

A. Reducing Costs

B. Identifying Security Vulnerabilities

C. Accelerating Migration

D. Ensuring Downtime

Answer: B - Identifying Security Vulnerabilities

Explanation: Pre-migration testing in server migration aims to identify security vulnerabilities and potential issues before the actual migration, ensuring a smoother transition.

Question 18:

Which cloud deployment characteristic allows resources to be provisioned and managed without human intervention?

A. On-Demand Self-Service

B. Broad Network Access

C. Rapid Elasticity

D. Measured Service

Answer: A - On-Demand Self-Service

Explanation: On-demand self-service in cloud deployment allows users to provision and manage resources without human intervention, promoting autonomy and efficiency.

Question 19:

What is the primary benefit of using measured service in cloud computing?

A. Ensuring Compatibility

B. Unlimited Access

C. Predictable Costs

D. Exclusive Contracts

Answer: C - Predictable Costs

Explanation: Measured service in cloud computing allows users to be billed based on actual usage, providing predictable and cost-effective pricing.

Question 20:

In cloud computing, what deployment model combines on-premises infrastructure with dedicated cloud resources for a single organization?

A. Public Cloud

B. Private Cloud

C. Hybrid Cloud

D. Community Cloud

Answer: C - Hybrid Cloud

Explanation: Hybrid clouds combine on-premises infrastructure with dedicated cloud resources, offering a flexible and scalable solution for a single organization.

Question 21:

Which characteristic allows cloud users to access services on a pay-as-you-go basis?

A. On-Demand Self-Service

B. Broad Network Access

C. Measured Service

D. Rapid Elasticity

Answer: C - Measured Service

Explanation: Measured service in cloud computing allows users to pay based on actual usage, ensuring a cost-effective pay-as-you-go model.

Question 22:

What deployment model involves multiple organizations sharing cloud resources based on common concerns, such as security or compliance?

A. Public Cloud

B. Private Cloud

C. Hybrid Cloud

D. Community Cloud

Answer: D - Community Cloud

Explanation: Community clouds involve multiple organizations sharing resources based on common concerns, fostering collaboration and addressing shared security or compliance requirements.

Question 23:

What is the primary role of load balancers in cloud computing?

A. Ensuring Compatibility

B. Improving Security

C. Efficient Resource Utilization

D. Distributing Workload

Answer: D - Distributing Workload

Explanation: Load balancers in cloud computing distribute incoming network traffic across multiple servers, ensuring efficient resource utilization and preventing overload on any single server.

Question 24:

Which characteristic allows cloud users to adjust resources automatically based on workload fluctuations?

A. On-Demand Self-Service

B. Broad Network Access

C. Rapid Elasticity

D. Measured Service

Answer: C - Rapid Elasticity

Explanation: Rapid elasticity allows cloud resources to automatically scale up or down based on workload fluctuations, ensuring flexibility and efficiency.

Question 25:

What deployment model is characterized by a cloud infrastructure shared by several organizations with common interests?

A. Public Cloud

B. Private Cloud

C. Hybrid Cloud

D. Community Cloud

Answer: D - Community Cloud

Explanation: Community clouds are shared by organizations with common interests, providing a collaborative and secure cloud infrastructure.

Chapter 3: Security in the Cloud

Cloud Security Compliance and Configurations

Ensuring robust security in the cloud is paramount for protecting sensitive data, maintaining compliance, and building trust in cloud services.

Compliance Frameworks:

Explore major compliance frameworks applicable to cloud environments, such as GDPR, HIPAA, and PCI DSS. Understand the importance of aligning cloud security practices with regulatory requirements and industry standards to mitigate risks and legal implications.

Security Configurations:

Learn best practices for configuring security settings in cloud platforms. Explore secure configuration guidelines for virtual machines, networks, and storage. Practical examples demonstrate the implementation of secure configurations to enhance the overall security posture.

Data Encryption:

Delve into the importance of data encryption in cloud security. Understand encryption protocols, key management, and the use of secure channels to protect data in transit and at rest. Case studies highlight the role of encryption in safeguarding sensitive information.

Incident Response and Reporting:

Develop a comprehensive incident response plan for addressing security incidents in the cloud. Explore reporting mechanisms, communication protocols, and the collaboration between cloud service providers and organizations during security incidents. Real-world scenarios illustrate effective incident response strategies.

Access Control

Effective access control is fundamental to maintaining the integrity and confidentiality of data in the cloud.

Identity and Access Management (IAM):

Delve into advanced concepts of IAM, including role-based access control (RBAC), attribute-based access control (ABAC), and fine-grained access policies. Understand how IAM contributes to enforcing the principle of least privilege and mitigating insider threats.

Multi-Factor Authentication (MFA):

Explore the significance of MFA in enhancing access security. Understand various MFA methods, their implementation, and their impact on preventing unauthorized access. Case studies showcase successful MFA deployments and their positive outcomes.

Privileged Access Management (PAM):

Learn about PAM and its role in securing privileged accounts. Understand the importance of monitoring and controlling access to critical systems and sensitive data. Practical guidance is provided for implementing PAM solutions to prevent unauthorized access and privilege misuse.

Access Monitoring and Auditing:

Explore access monitoring and auditing strategies to detect and respond to unauthorized activities. Understand the importance of logging, monitoring tools, and regular audits to ensure compliance and identify potential security incidents. Real-world examples illustrate the significance of proactive access monitoring.

By the end of this chapter, readers will have a comprehensive understanding of cloud security compliance, configurations, and access control. Each topic within this chapter equips readers with the knowledge and skills needed to implement robust security measures in the cloud, fostering a secure and trustworthy computing environment.

Practice Questions and Answers

Question 1:

Why is compliance with regulatory frameworks essential in cloud security?

A. Enhancing Performance

B. Legal Implications

C. Reducing Costs

D. Minimizing Downtime

Answer: B - Legal Implications

Explanation: Compliance with regulatory frameworks is essential in cloud security to mitigate legal implications and ensure adherence to industry standards.

Question 2:

What is the primary purpose of secure configuration settings in cloud platforms?

A. Improving User Experience

B. Minimizing Deployment Time

C. Enhancing Security

D. Reducing Storage Costs

Answer: C - Enhancing Security

Explanation: Secure configuration settings in cloud platforms are designed to enhance security by implementing best practices for virtual machines, networks, and storage.

Question 3:

Why is data encryption crucial in cloud security?

A. Improving User Experience

B. Reducing Storage Costs

C. Protecting Sensitive Data

D. Ensuring Compatibility

Answer: C - Protecting Sensitive Data

Explanation: Data encryption in cloud security is crucial for protecting sensitive data in transit and at rest, ensuring confidentiality and integrity.

Question 4:

What is the purpose of an incident response plan in cloud security?

A. Reducing Storage Costs

B. Enhancing Performance

C. Accelerating Deployment

D. Addressing Security Incidents

Answer: D - Addressing Security Incidents

Explanation: An incident response plan in cloud security is designed to address security incidents effectively, including detection, containment, eradication, and recovery.

Question 5:

Which compliance framework is focused on data protection and privacy for individuals within the European Union (EU)?

A. HIPAA

B. PCI DSS

C. GDPR

D. SOX

Answer: C - GDPR

Explanation: GDPR (General Data Protection Regulation) is a compliance framework focused on data protection and privacy for individuals within the European Union (EU).

Question 6:

What is the primary goal of identity and access management (IAM) in cloud security?

A. Reducing Storage Costs

B. Enhancing Performance

C. Ensuring Data Accessibility

D. Controlling Access

Answer: D - Controlling Access

Explanation: The primary goal of IAM in cloud security is to control access by implementing role-based access control (RBAC), attribute-based access control (ABAC), and fine-grained access policies.

Question 7:

Why is Multi-Factor Authentication (MFA) important in cloud access control?

A. Reducing Storage Costs

B. Enhancing Performance

C. Controlling Access

D. Increasing Complexity

Answer: C - Controlling Access

Explanation: MFA in cloud access control is important for controlling access by requiring multiple authentication factors, enhancing security.

Question 8:

What role does Privileged Access Management (PAM) play in cloud security?

A. Reducing Storage Costs

B. Enhancing Performance

C. Controlling Access to Critical Systems

D. Increasing User Autonomy

Answer: C - Controlling Access to Critical Systems

Explanation: PAM in cloud security plays a role in controlling access to critical systems and managing privileged accounts to prevent unauthorized access.

Question 9:

What is the primary benefit of access monitoring and auditing in cloud security?

A. Reducing Storage Costs

B. Enhancing Performance

C. Detecting Unauthorized Activities

D. Increasing User Autonomy

Answer: C - Detecting Unauthorized Activities

Explanation: Access monitoring and auditing in cloud security provide the primary benefit of detecting unauthorized activities and ensuring compliance through regular audits.

Question 10:

Which method is commonly used to protect data in transit in cloud security?

A. Virtual Private Network (VPN)

B. Data Encryption

C. Secure Sockets Layer (SSL)

D. Firewalls

Answer: C - Secure Sockets Layer (SSL)

Explanation: SSL is commonly used to protect data in transit by encrypting the communication between the client and server.

Question 11:

What does RBAC stand for in the context of cloud security?

A. Resource-Based Access Control

B. Role-Based Access Control

C. Role-Based Authorization Control

D. Resource-Based Authorization Control

Answer: B - Role-Based Access Control

Explanation: RBAC stands for Role-Based Access Control in the context of cloud security, where access is granted based on predefined roles.

Question 12:

What is the primary goal of attribute-based access control (ABAC) in cloud security?

A. Controlling Access

B. Improving User Experience

C. Minimizing Deployment Time

D. Ensuring Data Accessibility

Answer: A - Controlling Access

Explanation: The primary goal of ABAC in cloud security is to control access based on attributes such as user characteristics, roles, and environmental conditions.

Question 13:

Which authentication method involves verifying the identity of a user through something they know and something they have?

A. Single-Factor Authentication (SFA)

B. Multi-Factor Authentication (MFA)

C. Biometric Authentication

D. Token-based Authentication

Answer: B - Multi-Factor Authentication (MFA)

Explanation: MFA involves verifying the identity of a user through multiple factors, such as something they know (password) and something they have (token).

Question 14:

Why is fine-grained access control important in cloud security?

A. Reducing Storage Costs

B. Enhancing Performance

C. Controlling Access with Precision

D. Increasing User Autonomy

Answer: C - Controlling Access with Precision

Explanation: Fine-grained access control in cloud security is important for controlling access with precision by specifying detailed permissions based on user attributes and conditions.

Question 15:

What does GDPR focus on in the context of cloud security?

A. Global Data Protection

B. Governance and Risk Management

C. Data Protection and Privacy

D. Payment Card Industry Compliance

Answer: C - Data Protection and Privacy

Explanation: GDPR focuses on data protection and privacy, particularly for individuals within the European Union (EU), in the context of cloud security.

Question 16:

What is the primary purpose of secure channel protocols in cloud security?

A. Controlling Access

B. Enhancing Performance

C. Ensuring Data Integrity and Confidentiality

D. Increasing User Autonomy

Answer: C - Ensuring Data Integrity and Confidentiality

Explanation: Secure channel protocols in cloud security serve the primary purpose of ensuring data integrity and confidentiality during communication.

Question 17:

Which compliance framework is focused on ensuring the security of payment card transactions?

A. HIPAA

B. PCI DSS

C. GDPR

D. SOX

Answer: B - PCI DSS

Explanation: PCI DSS (Payment Card Industry Data Security Standard) is focused on ensuring the security of payment card transactions in the context of cloud security.

Question 18:

What is the primary goal of incident response in cloud security?

A. Reducing Storage Costs

B. Enhancing Performance

C. Addressing Security Incidents

D. Increasing User Autonomy

Answer: C - Addressing Security Incidents

Explanation: The primary goal of incident response in cloud security is to address security incidents effectively, including detection, containment, eradication, and recovery.

Question 19:

Which encryption key management practice ensures that the same key is not used for an extended period?

A. Key Rotation

B. Key Escrow

C. Key Generation

D. Key Revocation

Answer: A - Key Rotation

Explanation: Key rotation is an encryption key management practice that ensures that the same key is not used for an extended period, enhancing security.

Question 20:

What does PAM stand for in the context of cloud security?

A. Privileged Account Management

B. Protected Access Mechanism

C. Public Authentication Module

D. Protected Access Management

Answer: A - Privileged Account Management

Explanation: PAM stands for Privileged Account Management in the context of cloud security, focusing on managing access to privileged accounts.

Question 21:

Which access control method involves granting permissions based on user attributes and environmental conditions?

A. Role-Based Access Control (RBAC)

B. Attribute-Based Access Control (ABAC)

C. Least Privilege Access Control

D. Single-Factor Authentication (SFA)

Answer: B - Attribute-Based Access Control (ABAC)

Explanation: ABAC involves granting permissions based on user attributes and environmental conditions in the context of cloud security.

Question 22:

What is the primary benefit of regular audits in cloud security?

A. Reducing Storage Costs

B. Enhancing Performance

C. Detecting Unauthorized Activities

D. Increasing User Autonomy

Answer: C - Detecting Unauthorized Activities

Explanation: Regular audits in cloud security provide the primary benefit of detecting unauthorized activities and ensuring compliance through thorough monitoring.

Question 23:

Which authentication method involves verifying the identity of a user through unique physical or behavioral characteristics?

A. Single-Factor Authentication (SFA)

B. Multi-Factor Authentication (MFA)

C. Biometric Authentication

D. Token-based Authentication

Answer: C - Biometric Authentication

Explanation: Biometric authentication involves verifying the identity of a user through unique physical or behavioral characteristics, such as fingerprints or facial recognition.

Question 24:

What is the primary purpose of access monitoring in cloud security?

A. Reducing Storage Costs

B. Enhancing Performance

C. Detecting Unauthorized Activities

D. Increasing User Autonomy

Answer: C - Detecting Unauthorized Activities

Explanation: The primary purpose of access monitoring in cloud security is to detect unauthorized activities and ensure a proactive response to potential security incidents.

Question 25:

Which security concept ensures that users have access only to the resources and data necessary for their roles and responsibilities?

A. Least Privilege

B. Role-Based Access Control (RBAC)

C. Multi-Factor Authentication (MFA)

D. Secure Configuration

Answer: A - Least Privilege

Explanation: Least privilege ensures that users have access only to the resources and data necessary for their roles and responsibilities in the context of cloud security.

Chapter 4: Implementing Cloud Security

Implementing Security in the Cloud

Implementing robust security measures in the cloud is a dynamic and ongoing process that requires a combination of technical expertise, strategic planning, and continuous monitoring.

Security Best Practices:

Explore a comprehensive set of security best practices applicable to various cloud services, including infrastructure-as-a-service (IaaS), platform-as-a-service (PaaS), and software-as-a-service (SaaS). Understand how to configure security settings, manage access controls, and encrypt data to enhance overall security.

Network Security in the Cloud:

Delve into the intricacies of network security in the cloud, covering topics such as virtual private clouds (VPCs), firewalls, and intrusion detection and prevention systems. Learn how to design and implement secure network architectures to protect against unauthorized access and potential threats.

Container Security:

Understand the unique security considerations associated with containerized environments. Explore container orchestration platforms, secure container registries, and best practices for ensuring the integrity and isolation of containerized applications.

Security Monitoring and Incident Response:

Develop a proactive approach to security monitoring and incident response in the cloud. Explore the use of security information and event management (SIEM) tools, log analysis, and real-time monitoring to detect and respond to security incidents promptly.

Automating Cloud Security

Automation is a key enabler in implementing effective and scalable security measures in the cloud. This focuses on the automation of cloud security processes, allowing organizations to respond rapidly to evolving threats and maintain a secure environment.

Infrastructure as Code (IaC):

Explore the concept of Infrastructure as Code (IaC) and its role in automating the deployment and configuration of cloud resources. Learn how IaC templates can enhance consistency, reduce errors, and facilitate the rapid provisioning of secure infrastructure.

Continuous Integration and Continuous Deployment (CI/CD) Security:

Understand how to integrate security into the CI/CD pipeline to ensure that security measures are seamlessly incorporated throughout the development and deployment lifecycle. Explore automated testing, vulnerability scanning, and code analysis to identify and address security issues early in the development process.

Security Orchestration and Automation:

Delve into security orchestration and automation to streamline incident response and threat mitigation. Learn how to automate repetitive security tasks, integrate security tools, and orchestrate responses to security incidents for efficient and effective risk management.

Cloud Security Policies and Compliance Automation:

Explore the automation of cloud security policies and compliance checks. Understand how automated tools can continuously assess adherence to security policies, regulatory requirements, and industry standards, enabling organizations to maintain a compliant and secure posture.

Practice Questions And Answers

Question 1:

What is a fundamental consideration when implementing security in a cloud environment?

A. Maximizing Costs

B. Ensuring 100% Uptime

C. Adhering to Best Practices

D. Ignoring Access Controls

Answer: C - Adhering to Best Practices

Explanation: Adhering to security best practices is fundamental when implementing security in a cloud environment to enhance overall security posture.

Question 2:

Why is network security crucial in a cloud environment?

A. Enhancing User Experience

B. Minimizing Deployment Time

C. Protecting Against Unauthorized Access and Threats

D. Reducing Storage Costs

Answer: C - Protecting Against Unauthorized Access and Threats

Explanation: Network security in a cloud environment is crucial for protecting against unauthorized access and potential threats to ensure the integrity of data and resources.

Question 3:

What is the purpose of a virtual private cloud (VPC) in cloud security?

A. Enhancing User Experience

B. Isolating Network Traffic

C. Reducing Storage Costs

D. Minimizing Deployment Time

Answer: B - Isolating Network Traffic

Explanation: A virtual private cloud (VPC) in cloud security is designed to isolate and control network traffic, providing a secure and isolated network environment.

Question 4:

Why is Infrastructure as Code (IaC) considered beneficial in cloud security?

A. Increasing Complexity

B. Reducing Deployment Time

C. Ignoring Security Best Practices

D. Maximizing Costs

Answer: B - Reducing Deployment Time

Explanation: Infrastructure as Code (IaC) is beneficial in cloud security for reducing deployment time, enhancing consistency, and minimizing errors in infrastructure provisioning.

Question 5:

What is the primary goal of continuous integration and continuous deployment (CI/CD) security?

A. Minimizing Deployment Time

B. Ensuring 100% Uptime

C. Integrating Security Throughout the Development Lifecycle

D. Reducing Storage Costs

Answer: C - Integrating Security Throughout the Development Lifecycle

Explanation: CI/CD security aims to integrate security measures seamlessly throughout the development and deployment lifecycle to identify and address security issues early.

Question 6:

What is the purpose of container orchestration platforms in cloud security?

A. Reducing Storage Costs

B. Minimizing Deployment Time

C. Enhancing Security and Isolation of Containerized Applications

D. Ignoring Security Best Practices

Answer: C - Enhancing Security and Isolation of Containerized Applications

Explanation: Container orchestration platforms in cloud security enhance the security and isolation of containerized applications, ensuring integrity and reliability.

Question 7:

What role does security information and event management (SIEM) play in cloud security?

A. Reducing Deployment Time

B. Enhancing User Experience

C. Proactive Security Monitoring and Incident Response

D. Maximizing Costs

Answer: C - Proactive Security Monitoring and Incident Response

Explanation: SIEM in cloud security contributes to proactive security monitoring and incident response by analyzing security events and providing real-time insights.

Question 8:

Why is privileged access management (PAM) important in cloud security?

A. Maximizing Costs

B. Ensuring 100% Uptime

C. Controlling Access to Critical Systems and Data

D. Reducing Storage Costs

Answer: C - Controlling Access to Critical Systems and Data

Explanation: PAM in cloud security is important for controlling access to critical systems and data, preventing unauthorized access and privilege misuse.

Question 9:

What does security orchestration and automation aim to achieve?

A. Reducing Deployment Time

B. Enhancing User Experience

C. Streamlining Incident Response and Threat Mitigation

D. Maximizing Costs

Answer: C - Streamlining Incident Response and Threat Mitigation

Explanation: Security orchestration and automation aim to streamline incident response and threat mitigation in cloud security, automating repetitive tasks for efficiency.

Question 10:

How does automated testing contribute to cloud security in the CI/CD pipeline?

A. Reducing Deployment Time

B. Ensuring 100% Uptime

C. Identifying and Addressing Security Issues Early

D. Ignoring Security Best Practices

Answer: C - Identifying and Addressing Security Issues Early

Explanation: Automated testing in the CI/CD pipeline contributes to cloud security by identifying and addressing security issues early in the development process.

Question 11:

What is the primary goal of security monitoring in a cloud environment?

A. Minimizing Deployment Time

B. Enhancing User Experience

C. Detecting and Responding to Security Incidents

D. Maximizing Costs

Answer: C - Detecting and Responding to Security Incidents

Explanation: The primary goal of security monitoring in a cloud environment is to detect and respond to security incidents promptly.

Question 12:

Why is encryption important in cloud security?

A. Increasing Complexity

B. Ensuring 100% Uptime

C. Protecting Sensitive Data in Transit and at Rest

D. Reducing Storage Costs

Answer: C - Protecting Sensitive Data in Transit and at Rest

Explanation: Encryption in cloud security is important for protecting sensitive data in transit and at rest, ensuring confidentiality and integrity.

Question 13:

What is the significance of secure container registries in cloud security?

A. Reducing Storage Costs

B. Minimizing Deployment Time

C. Ensuring the Integrity and Origin of Container Images

D. Ignoring Security Best Practices

Answer: C - Ensuring the Integrity and Origin of Container Images

Explanation: Secure container registries in cloud security ensure the integrity and origin of container images, preventing tampering or unauthorized modifications.

Question 14:

Why is access monitoring important in a cloud environment?

A. Minimizing Deployment Time

B. Enhancing User Experience

C. Detecting Unauthorized Activities

D. Reducing Storage Costs

Answer: C - Detecting Unauthorized Activities

Explanation: Access monitoring in a cloud environment is important for detecting unauthorized activities and ensuring compliance through thorough monitoring.

Question 15:

What is the primary benefit of security policies and compliance automation in cloud security?

A. Reducing Deployment Time

B. Enhancing User Experience

C. Ensuring Continuous Adherence to Security Policies and Standards

D. Maximizing Costs

Answer: C - Ensuring Continuous Adherence to Security Policies and Standards

Explanation: Security policies and compliance automation in cloud security ensure continuous adherence to security policies and standards, reducing the risk of non-compliance.

Question 16:

How does automation contribute to reducing errors in cloud security?

A. Increasing Complexity

B. Ensuring 100% Uptime

C. Enhancing Consistency and Minimizing Human Errors

D. Reducing Storage Costs

Answer: C - Enhancing Consistency and Minimizing Human Errors

Explanation: Automation in cloud security enhances consistency and minimizes human errors, contributing to the reduction of errors in security configurations and processes.

Question 17:

What is the primary purpose of intrusion detection and prevention systems (IDPS) in network security?

A. Minimizing Deployment Time

B. Enhancing User Experience

C. Detecting and Preventing Unauthorized Access and Threats

D. Maximizing Costs

Answer: C - Detecting and Preventing Unauthorized Access and Threats

Explanation: IDPS in network security plays a primary role in detecting and preventing unauthorized access and potential threats to the network.

Question 18:

How can cloud security benefit from automated incident response?

A. Reducing Deployment Time

B. Ensuring 100% Uptime

C. Rapidly Responding to Security Incidents

D. Ignoring Security Best Practices

Answer: C - Rapidly Responding to Security Incidents

Explanation: Automated incident response in cloud security enables rapid responses to security incidents, reducing the impact and minimizing downtime.

Question 19:

What is the role of firewalls in cloud network security?

A. Reducing Storage Costs

B. Minimizing Deployment Time

C. Monitoring Network Traffic

D. Ignoring Security Best Practices

Answer: C - Monitoring Network Traffic

Explanation: Firewalls in cloud network security play a role in monitoring and controlling network traffic, preventing unauthorized access and potential threats.

Question 20:

How can automated tools assist in ensuring compliance in cloud security?

A. Minimizing Deployment Time

B. Enhancing User Experience

C. Continuously Assessing Adherence to Security Policies and Standards

D. Maximizing Costs

Answer: C - Continuously Assessing Adherence to Security Policies and Standards

Explanation: Automated tools in cloud security assist in ensuring compliance by continuously assessing adherence to security policies and standards.

Question 21:

What is the primary goal of container security in cloud environments?

A. Minimizing Deployment Time

B. Enhancing User Experience

C. Ensuring the Integrity and Isolation of Containerized Applications

D. Reducing Storage Costs

Answer: C - Ensuring the Integrity and Isolation of Containerized Applications

Explanation: The primary goal of container security in cloud environments is to ensure the integrity and isolation of containerized applications, preventing security vulnerabilities.

Question 22:

How does multi-cloud security differ from single-cloud security implementation?

A. Increasing Complexity

B. Ensuring 100% Uptime

C. Managing Security Across Multiple Cloud Providers

D. Ignoring Security Best Practices

Answer: C - Managing Security Across Multiple Cloud Providers

Explanation: Multi-cloud security differs from single-cloud security by requiring the management of security measures across multiple cloud providers.

Question 23:

What is the significance of secure channels in cloud security?

A. Reducing Storage Costs

B. Minimizing Deployment Time

C. Ensuring Confidentiality and Integrity of Data in Transit

D. Ignoring Security Best Practices

Answer: C - Ensuring Confidentiality and Integrity of Data in Transit

Explanation: Secure channels in cloud security ensure the confidentiality and integrity of data in transit by encrypting communication between clients and servers.

Question 24:

Why is identity and access management (IAM) crucial in cloud security?

A. Minimizing Deployment Time

B. Ensuring 100% Uptime

C. Controlling Access and Implementing Least Privilege

D. Reducing Storage Costs

Answer: C - Controlling Access and Implementing Least Privilege

Explanation: IAM in cloud security is crucial for controlling access and implementing the principle of least privilege, ensuring users have access only to necessary resources.

Question 25:

How does cloud security benefit from automation in access control?

A. Reducing Storage Costs

B. Minimizing Deployment Time

C. Efficiently Managing and Enforcing Access Policies

D. Ignoring Security Best Practices

Answer: C - Efficiently Managing and Enforcing Access Policies

Explanation: Automation in access control in cloud security enables efficient management and enforcement of access policies, reducing the risk of human errors.

Chapter 5: Maintaining Cloud Operations

Applying Security Patches

Keeping cloud systems secure is an ongoing process that involves timely application of security patches. This part focuses on the importance of applying security patches and the best practices for maintaining a secure and resilient cloud infrastructure.

Patch Management Process:

Explore the patch management lifecycle, from vulnerability identification to testing and deployment. Understand the significance of a well-defined patch management process in mitigating security risks and vulnerabilities.

Automated Patching Tools:

Delve into the use of automated patching tools to streamline the patching process. Learn how these tools can enhance efficiency, reduce downtime, and ensure that security patches are applied consistently across the cloud environment.

Risk Assessment and Prioritization:

Understand the importance of conducting risk assessments and prioritizing patches based on criticality. Explore methods for evaluating the potential impact of patches on system stability and performance.

Continuous Monitoring and Reporting:

Learn how continuous monitoring and reporting contribute to the effectiveness of patch management. Explore tools and practices for tracking patch status, identifying vulnerabilities, and generating reports for stakeholders.

Updating Cloud Elements

The cloud environment consists of various elements, including virtual machines, databases, and networking components. This focuses on the importance of regularly updating these elements to ensure optimal performance, reliability, and security.

Virtual Machine Updates:

Explore best practices for updating virtual machines, including operating systems, software applications, and dependencies. Understand the impact of updates on system performance and how to minimize disruptions during the update process.

Database Maintenance and Updates:

Delve into the maintenance and update procedures for cloud databases. Learn about backup strategies, database optimization, and the importance of applying database software updates to address security vulnerabilities and enhance performance.

Networking Element Updates:

Understand the significance of updating networking elements, such as routers, firewalls, and load balancers. Explore practices for minimizing downtime, ensuring compatibility, and implementing updates without compromising network security.

Storage Operations

Efficient and secure storage operations are crucial for maintaining data integrity and availability in the cloud. This covers various aspects of storage operations, including data backup, disaster recovery, and storage optimization.

Data Backup Strategies:

Explore effective strategies for backing up data in the cloud, including regular backups, incremental backups, and offsite backups. Understand the importance of data redundancy and the role of automated backup solutions.

Disaster Recovery Planning:

Delve into disaster recovery planning for cloud storage. Learn how to create comprehensive disaster recovery plans, including data recovery objectives, backup testing, and the implementation of failover and failback procedures.

Storage Optimization Techniques:

Understand storage optimization techniques to maximize the efficiency of cloud storage. Explore deduplication, compression, and tiered storage strategies to reduce costs and enhance overall storage performance.

By the end of this chapter, readers will have gained insights into the critical aspects of maintaining cloud operations, including applying security patches, updating various cloud elements, and optimizing storage operations. Each section provides practical guidance for organizations aiming to establish a robust and resilient cloud infrastructure.

Practice Questions And Answers

Question 1:

What is the primary goal of a patch management process in cloud operations?

A. Enhancing User Experience

B. Reducing Storage Costs

C. Mitigating Security Risks and Vulnerabilities

D. Maximizing Costs

Answer: C - Mitigating Security Risks and Vulnerabilities

Explanation: The primary goal of a patch management process is to mitigate security risks and vulnerabilities in cloud operations.

Question 2:

Why is risk assessment and prioritization crucial in the patch management lifecycle?

A. Ignoring Security Best Practices

B. Enhancing User Experience

C. Identifying Critical Patches

D. Reducing Deployment Time

Answer: C - Identifying Critical Patches

Explanation: Risk assessment and prioritization are crucial for identifying critical patches and prioritizing their deployment to address high-impact vulnerabilities.

Question 3:

How do automated patching tools contribute to efficient cloud operations?

A. Increasing Complexity

B. Reducing Deployment Time

C. Ignoring Security Best Practices

D. Maximizing Costs

Answer: B - Reducing Deployment Time

Explanation: Automated patching tools contribute to efficient cloud operations by reducing deployment time and ensuring consistent application of patches.

Question 4:

What role does continuous monitoring play in the effectiveness of patch management?

A. Ignoring Security Best Practices

B. Enhancing User Experience

C. Tracking Patch Status and Identifying Vulnerabilities

D. Reducing Storage Costs

Answer: C - Tracking Patch Status and Identifying Vulnerabilities

Explanation: Continuous monitoring is essential for tracking patch status, identifying vulnerabilities, and ensuring the effectiveness of patch management.

Question 5:

Why is it important to conduct risk assessments before applying security patches?

A. Ignoring Security Best Practices

B. Reducing Deployment Time

C. Evaluating Potential Impact on System Stability and Performance

D. Maximizing Costs

Answer: C - Evaluating Potential Impact on System Stability and Performance

Explanation: Risk assessments are important for evaluating the potential impact of security patches on system stability and performance before deployment.

Question 6:

What is a best practice for updating virtual machines in cloud operations?

A. Ignoring Security Best Practices

B. Maximizing Costs

C. Minimizing Disruptions During the Update Process

D. Reducing Deployment Time

Answer: C - Minimizing Disruptions During the Update Process

Explanation: A best practice for updating virtual machines is to minimize disruptions during the update process, ensuring continuous operation.

Question 7:

Why is updating cloud databases important for security and performance?

A. Ignoring Security Best Practices

B. Reducing Deployment Time

C. Addressing Security Vulnerabilities and Enhancing Performance

D. Maximizing Costs

Answer: C - Addressing Security Vulnerabilities and Enhancing Performance

Explanation: Updating cloud databases is important for addressing security vulnerabilities and enhancing overall performance in cloud operations.

Question 8:

What role do networking element updates play in cloud operations?

A. Ignoring Security Best Practices

B. Reducing Deployment Time

C. Ensuring Compatibility and Enhancing Security

D. Maximizing Costs

Answer: C - Ensuring Compatibility and Enhancing Security

Explanation: Networking element updates in cloud operations ensure compatibility and enhance security by addressing potential vulnerabilities.

Question 9:

How can updates be applied to networking elements without compromising security?

A. Ignoring Security Best Practices

B. Minimizing Downtime and Implementing Security Measures

C. Maximizing Costs

D. Reducing Deployment Time

Answer: B - Minimizing Downtime and Implementing Security Measures

Explanation: Updates to networking elements should be applied with measures to minimize downtime and implement security measures to avoid compromising security.

Question 10:

What is the significance of updating networking components like routers and firewalls in cloud operations?

A. Ignoring Security Best Practices

B. Reducing Deployment Time

C. Maintaining a Secure Network Environment

D. Maximizing Costs

Answer: C - Maintaining a Secure Network Environment

Explanation: Updating networking components is significant for maintaining a secure network environment in cloud operations.

Question 11:

Why is data backup considered a critical strategy in cloud storage operations?

A. Ignoring Security Best Practices

B. Reducing Deployment Time

C. Minimizing Data Loss and Ensuring Business Continuity

D. Maximizing Costs

Answer: C - Minimizing Data Loss and Ensuring Business Continuity

Explanation: Data backup is a critical strategy in cloud storage operations to minimize data loss and ensure business continuity.

Question 12:

What is the primary purpose of disaster recovery planning in cloud storage operations?

A. Ignoring Security Best Practices

B. Reducing Deployment Time

C. Ensuring Rapid Recovery in the Event of Data Loss or System Failures

D. Maximizing Costs

Answer: C - Ensuring Rapid Recovery in the Event of Data Loss or System Failures

Explanation: Disaster recovery planning in cloud storage operations ensures rapid recovery in the event of data loss or system failures.

Question 13:

How can data recovery objectives contribute to effective disaster recovery in cloud storage operations?

A. Ignoring Security Best Practices

B. Defining Timeframes for Data Recovery

C. Maximizing Costs

D. Reducing Deployment Time

Answer: B - Defining Timeframes for Data Recovery

Explanation: Data recovery objectives contribute to effective disaster recovery by defining timeframes for data recovery in cloud storage operations.

Question 14:

What role does automated backup solutions play in cloud storage operations?

A. Ignoring Security Best Practices

B. Reducing Deployment Time

C. Ensuring Regular and Consistent Data Backups

D. Maximizing Costs

Answer: C - Ensuring Regular and Consistent Data Backups

Explanation: Automated backup solutions play a role in cloud storage operations by ensuring regular and consistent data backups.

Question 15:

Why is storage optimization crucial in cloud storage operations?

A. Ignoring Security Best Practices

B. Reducing Deployment Time

C. Maximizing Costs

D. Efficiently Utilizing Storage Resources

Answer: D - Efficiently Utilizing Storage Resources

Explanation: Storage optimization is crucial in cloud storage operations for efficiently utilizing storage resources and minimizing costs.

Question 16:

What storage optimization technique focuses on reducing redundant data in cloud storage?

A. Ignoring Security Best Practices

B. Compression

C. Deduplication

D. Maximizing Costs

Answer: C - Deduplication

Explanation: Deduplication is a storage optimization technique that focuses on reducing redundant data in cloud storage.

Question 17:

How does tiered storage contribute to cost-effective cloud storage operations?

A. Ignoring Security Best Practices

B. Reducing Deployment Time

C. Ensuring Optimal Performance for Different Types of Data

D. Maximizing Costs

Answer: C - Ensuring Optimal Performance for Different Types of Data

Explanation: Tiered storage contributes to cost-effective cloud storage operations by ensuring optimal performance for different types of data based on their importance.

Question 18:

Why is continuous monitoring essential in storage operations in the cloud?

A. Ignoring Security Best Practices

B. Reducing Deployment Time

C. Detecting Anomalies and Ensuring Data Availability

D. Maximizing Costs

Answer: C - Detecting Anomalies and Ensuring Data Availability

Explanation: Continuous monitoring is essential in storage operations to detect anomalies and ensure data availability in the cloud.

Question 19:

What is the primary goal of storage optimization in cloud operations?

A. Ignoring Security Best Practices

B. Reducing Deployment Time

C. Maximizing Costs

D. Improving Efficiency and Reducing Wastage of Storage Resources

Answer: D - Improving Efficiency and Reducing Wastage of Storage Resources

Explanation: The primary goal of storage optimization is to improve efficiency and reduce wastage of storage resources in cloud operations.

Question 20:

How can compression contribute to storage optimization in cloud operations?

A. Ignoring Security Best Practices

B. Reducing Deployment Time

C. Minimizing Storage Space by Compressing Data

D. Maximizing Costs

Answer: C - Minimizing Storage Space by Compressing Data

Explanation: Compression contributes to storage optimization by minimizing storage space through the compression of data in cloud operations.

Question 21:

How can automated patching tools help in maintaining a secure cloud environment?

A. Ignoring Security Best Practices

B. Reducing Deployment Time

C. Increasing Complexity

D. Maximizing Costs

Answer: B - Reducing Deployment Time

Explanation: Automated patching tools help in maintaining a secure cloud environment by reducing deployment time and ensuring efficient and consistent patch application.

Question 22:

Why is it crucial to test patches before deploying them in a cloud environment?

A. Ignoring Security Best Practices

B. Reducing Deployment Time

C. Minimizing Potential Disruptions and Compatibility Issues

D. Maximizing Costs

Answer: C - Minimizing Potential Disruptions and Compatibility Issues

Explanation: Testing patches before deployment is crucial to minimize potential disruptions and address compatibility issues in a cloud environment.

Question 23:

What is the role of risk assessments in the patch management process?

A. Ignoring Security Best Practices

B. Identifying Critical Patches and Prioritizing Deployment

C. Maximizing Costs

D. Reducing Deployment Time

Answer: B - Identifying Critical Patches and Prioritizing Deployment

Explanation: Risk assessments in the patch management process help identify critical patches and prioritize their deployment based on potential impact.

Question 24:

How does continuous monitoring contribute to the security of a cloud environment?

A. Ignoring Security Best Practices

B. Reducing Deployment Time

C. Detecting and Responding to Security Incidents

D. Maximizing Costs

Answer: C - Detecting and Responding to Security Incidents

Explanation: Continuous monitoring contributes to the security of a cloud environment by detecting and responding to security incidents in real-time.

Question 25:

What challenges might organizations face in the continuous monitoring of patch status and vulnerabilities in a large-scale cloud environment?

A. Ignoring Security Best Practices

B. Increasing Complexity

C. Reducing Deployment Time

D. Maximizing Costs

Answer: B - Increasing Complexity

Explanation: Continuous monitoring challenges in a large-scale cloud environment may include increased complexity due to the vast number of resources and configurations.

Question 26:

Why is it important to minimize disruptions during the update process of virtual machines in cloud operations?

A. Ignoring Security Best Practices

B. Maximizing Costs

C. Ensuring Continuous Operation and User Experience

D. Reducing Deployment Time

Answer: C - Ensuring Continuous Operation and User Experience

Explanation: Minimizing disruptions during the update process of virtual machines is important to ensure continuous operation and a positive user experience in cloud operations.

Question 27:

What factors should be considered when updating cloud databases for optimal security and performance?

A. Ignoring Security Best Practices

B. Reducing Deployment Time

C. Addressing Security Vulnerabilities and Optimizing Database Performance

D. Maximizing Costs

Answer: C - Addressing Security Vulnerabilities and Optimizing Database Performance

Explanation: When updating cloud databases, factors like addressing security vulnerabilities and optimizing database performance should be considered for optimal security and performance.

Question 28:

How can organizations ensure the compatibility of networking element updates with existing configurations in cloud operations?

A. Ignoring Security Best Practices

B. Reducing Deployment Time

C. Testing Updates in a Controlled Environment and Ensuring Compatibility

D. Maximizing Costs

Answer: C - Testing Updates in a Controlled Environment and Ensuring Compatibility

Explanation: Organizations can ensure compatibility by testing updates in a controlled environment before deploying them in cloud operations.

Question 29:

What is the primary goal of updating networking components like routers and firewalls in a cloud environment?

A. Ignoring Security Best Practices

B. Reducing Deployment Time

C. Ensuring Compatibility and Enhancing Security

D. Maximizing Costs

Answer: C - Ensuring Compatibility and Enhancing Security

Explanation: The primary goal of updating networking components is to ensure compatibility and enhance security in a cloud environment.

Question 30:

How can organizations minimize downtime during the update process of networking elements in cloud operations?

A. Ignoring Security Best Practices

B. Maximizing Costs

C. Implementing Redundancy and Failover Mechanisms

D. Reducing Deployment Time

Answer: C - Implementing Redundancy and Failover Mechanisms

Explanation: Organizations can minimize downtime by implementing redundancy and failover mechanisms during the update process of networking elements in cloud operations.

Question 31:

Why should organizations conduct regular backups in cloud storage operations?

A. Ignoring Security Best Practices

B. Reducing Deployment Time

C. Ensuring Data Availability and Minimizing Data Loss

D. Maximizing Costs

Answer: C - Ensuring Data Availability and Minimizing Data Loss

Explanation: Regular backups in cloud storage operations ensure data availability and minimize the risk of data loss in case of unforeseen events.

Question 32:

What is the significance of defining data recovery objectives in disaster recovery planning for cloud storage operations?

A. Ignoring Security Best Practices

B. Reducing Deployment Time

C. Maximizing Costs

D. Establishing Clear Timeframes for Data Recovery

Answer: D - Establishing Clear Timeframes for Data Recovery

Explanation: Defining data recovery objectives helps establish clear timeframes for data recovery in disaster recovery planning for cloud storage operations.

Question 33:

How do automated backup solutions contribute to the efficiency of data backup in cloud storage operations?

A. Ignoring Security Best Practices

B. Reducing Deployment Time

C. Ensuring Regular and Consistent Data Backups

D. Maximizing Costs

Answer: C - Ensuring Regular and Consistent Data Backups

Explanation: Automated backup solutions contribute to the efficiency of data backup by ensuring regular and consistent backups in cloud storage operations.

Question 34:

What challenges might organizations face in implementing a tiered storage strategy in cloud operations?

A. Ignoring Security Best Practices

B. Increasing Complexity

C. Reducing Deployment Time

D. Maximizing Costs

Answer: B - Increasing Complexity

Explanation: Organizations may face challenges related to increased complexity when implementing a tiered storage strategy in cloud operations.

Question 35:

How does storage optimization contribute to cost savings in cloud storage operations?

A. Ignoring Security Best Practices

B. Reducing Deployment Time

C. Maximizing Costs

D. Efficiently Utilizing Storage Resources

Answer: D - Efficiently Utilizing Storage Resources

Explanation: Storage optimization contributes to cost savings in cloud storage operations by efficiently utilizing storage resources and minimizing unnecessary costs.

Question 36:

What is the primary purpose of deduplication in storage optimization in cloud operations?

A. Ignoring Security Best Practices

B. Compression of Data

C. Reducing Deployment Time

D. Minimizing Storage Space by Reducing Redundant Data

Answer: D - Minimizing Storage Space by Reducing Redundant Data

Explanation: Deduplication in storage optimization aims to minimize storage space by reducing redundant data in cloud operations.

Question 37:

How can organizations ensure the effectiveness of disaster recovery plans in cloud storage operations?

A. Ignoring Security Best Practices

B. Regularly Testing and Updating Disaster Recovery Plans

C. Maximizing Costs

D. Reducing Deployment Time

Answer: B - Regularly Testing and Updating Disaster Recovery Plans

Explanation: Regular testing and updating of disaster recovery plans help ensure their effectiveness in cloud storage operations.

Question 38:

Why is continuous monitoring essential for detecting anomalies in storage operations in the cloud?

A. Ignoring Security Best Practices

B. Reducing Deployment Time

C. Detecting Anomalies and Ensuring Data Availability

D. Maximizing Costs

Answer: C - Detecting Anomalies and Ensuring Data Availability

Explanation: Continuous monitoring is essential for detecting anomalies and ensuring data availability in storage operations in the cloud.

Question 39:

What benefits can organizations derive from efficiently utilizing storage resources in cloud operations?

A. Ignoring Security Best Practices

B. Reducing Deployment Time

C. Maximizing Costs

D. Cost Savings and Improved Operational Efficiency

Answer: D - Cost Savings and Improved Operational Efficiency

Explanation: Efficiently utilizing storage resources in cloud operations leads to cost savings and improved operational efficiency for organizations.

Question 40:

How does compression contribute to storage optimization in cloud operations?

A. Ignoring Security Best Practices

B. Reducing Deployment Time

C. Maximizing Costs

D. Minimizing Storage Space by Compressing Data

Answer: D - Minimizing Storage Space by Compressing Data

Explanation: Compression contributes to storage optimization by minimizing storage space through the compression of data in cloud operations.

Chapter 6: Disaster Recovery, Business Continuity, and Ongoing Maintenance

Implementing a Disaster Recovery and Business Continuity Plan

Detailed insights into the planning process, encompassing risk assessments, defining recovery objectives, and creating comprehensive plans to minimize downtime and data loss during unexpected disruptions.

Cloud-specific Considerations:

Understanding how cloud-specific factors, such as data replication, backup strategies, and geographical redundancy, play a pivotal role in enhancing the effectiveness of a DR and BC plan in the cloud.

Testing and Validation:

Emphasis on the importance of regularly testing and validating the DR and BC plan to ensure its readiness. Practical guidance on conducting simulated drills and exercises to identify and address potential gaps.

Communication Protocols:

Establishing clear communication protocols for stakeholders during a disaster scenario. Strategies for effective communication, both internally and externally, to minimize confusion and ensure a coordinated response.

Business Continuity

This delves deeper into the concept of business continuity, emphasizing its significance beyond disaster recovery.

Operational Resilience:

Exploring strategies for building operational resilience, including redundancy in critical systems, resource allocation, and contingency planning to maintain business operations during disruptions.

Employee Training and Awareness:

The role of employee training and awareness in business continuity. Strategies for educating and preparing employees to respond effectively to disruptions, ensuring a cohesive and coordinated effort.

Supply Chain Continuity:

Understanding the impact of disruptions on the supply chain and implementing measures to ensure continuity. Strategies for identifying and mitigating risks within the supply chain in a cloud-centric business environment.

Cloud Maintenance

This focuses on the ongoing maintenance of cloud environments to ensure optimal performance, security, and cost-effectiveness.

Performance Monitoring and Optimization:

Strategies for monitoring and optimizing cloud performance. Utilizing tools and best practices to identify bottlenecks, optimize resource utilization, and enhance overall system performance.

Security Updates and Compliance:

The importance of regularly updating security measures in the cloud. Strategies for staying compliant with industry standards and addressing security vulnerabilities to maintain a secure cloud environment.

Cost Management and Resource Efficiency:

Practical approaches to managing costs and maximizing resource efficiency in the cloud. Understanding cost structures, implementing cost controls, and optimizing resource allocation to ensure cost-effective cloud operations.

Scaling Strategies:

Exploring scaling strategies in the cloud, including vertical and horizontal scaling. Understanding when and how to scale resources to meet changing demands and ensure the scalability of cloud infrastructure.

By the end of this chapter, readers will have a comprehensive understanding of disaster recovery, business continuity, and ongoing maintenance specific to cloud environments. Practical insights and actionable strategies will equip them to navigate challenges and build resilient cloud-based systems.

Practice Questions and Answers

Question 1:

What is the first step in implementing a disaster recovery and business continuity plan for cloud environments?

A. Conducting Risk Assessments

B. Creating Communication Protocols

C. Testing and Validating the Plan

D. Establishing Redundant Data Centers

Answer: A - Conducting Risk Assessments

Explanation: The first step is to conduct risk assessments to identify potential threats and vulnerabilities.

Question 2:

Why are cloud-specific considerations essential when designing a disaster recovery plan?

A. To Ignore Traditional DR Strategies

B. To Address Unique Challenges and Opportunities

C. To Increase Deployment Time

D. To Maximize Costs

Answer: B - To Address Unique Challenges and Opportunities

Explanation: Cloud-specific considerations help tailor the disaster recovery plan to address the unique challenges and opportunities presented by cloud environments.

Question 3:

What is the purpose of testing and validating a disaster recovery plan?

A. To Increase Deployment Time

B. To Ignore Security Best Practices

C. To Identify and Address Potential Gaps

D. To Maximize Costs

Answer: C - To Identify and Address Potential Gaps

Explanation: Testing and validation help identify and address potential gaps in the disaster recovery plan, ensuring its effectiveness during actual disruptions.

Question 4:

How do communication protocols contribute to effective disaster recovery and business continuity?

A. By Increasing Complexity

B. By Minimizing Confusion and Ensuring a Coordinated Response

C. By Ignoring Security Best Practices

D. By Maximizing Costs

Answer: B - By Minimizing Confusion and Ensuring a Coordinated Response

Explanation: Communication protocols minimize confusion and ensure a coordinated response among stakeholders during a disaster scenario.

Question 5:

What role does geographical redundancy play in cloud disaster recovery planning?

A. Ignoring Security Best Practices

B. Minimizing Costs

C. Ensuring Data Availability and Reducing Downtime

D. Maximizing Deployment Time

Answer: C - Ensuring Data Availability and Reducing Downtime

Explanation: Geographical redundancy ensures data availability and reduces downtime by replicating data across multiple geographic locations.

Question 6:

How can organizations ensure the readiness of their disaster recovery plan?

A. Ignoring Security Best Practices

B. Regularly Testing and Updating the Plan

C. Maximizing Costs

D. Reducing Deployment Time

Answer: B - Regularly Testing and Updating the Plan

Explanation: Organizations can ensure the readiness of their disaster recovery plan by regularly testing and updating it to address evolving threats and changes in the environment.

Question 7:

What is the primary goal of a business continuity plan beyond disaster recovery?

A. Ignoring Security Best Practices

B. Minimizing Costs

C. Maintaining Business Operations During Disruptions

D. Maximizing Deployment Time

Answer: C - Maintaining Business Operations During Disruptions

Explanation: The primary goal of a business continuity plan is to maintain business operations during disruptions beyond traditional disaster recovery efforts.

Question 8:

How can employee training and awareness contribute to effective business continuity?

A. Ignoring Security Best Practices

B. Reducing Deployment Time

C. Ensuring a Cohesive and Coordinated Response

D. Maximizing Costs

Answer: C - Ensuring a Cohesive and Coordinated Response

Explanation: Employee training and awareness ensure a cohesive and coordinated response during disruptions, minimizing the impact on business operations.

Question 9:

Why is supply chain continuity essential for business continuity in cloud-centric environments?

A. Ignoring Security Best Practices

B. Maximizing Costs

C. Minimizing Disruptions to Operations

D. Reducing Deployment Time

Answer: C - Minimizing Disruptions to Operations

Explanation: Supply chain continuity minimizes disruptions to operations by ensuring the uninterrupted flow of goods and services in cloud-centric environments.

Question 10:

How does operational resilience differ from traditional disaster recovery planning?

A. Ignoring Security Best Practices

B. Focusing on Maintaining Operations Rather Than Just Recovery

C. Maximizing Costs

D. Reducing Deployment Time

Answer: B - Focusing on Maintaining Operations Rather Than Just Recovery

Explanation: Operational resilience focuses on maintaining operations rather than just recovery, encompassing a broader range of strategies beyond traditional disaster recovery planning.

Question 11:

What measures can organizations take to build operational resilience in cloud environments?

A. Ignoring Security Best Practices

B. Establishing Redundancy in Critical Systems

C. Maximizing Costs

D. Reducing Deployment Time

Answer: B - Establishing Redundancy in Critical Systems

Explanation: Organizations can build operational resilience by establishing redundancy in critical systems to ensure continuity of operations during disruptions.

Question 12:

How does employee training contribute to effective business continuity?

A. Ignoring Security Best Practices

B. Reducing Deployment Time

C. Enhancing Preparedness and Response Capabilities

D. Maximizing Costs

Answer: C - Enhancing Preparedness and Response Capabilities

Explanation: Employee training enhances preparedness and response capabilities, enabling a more effective response during disruptions in business continuity.

Question 13:

What strategies can organizations implement to maintain supply chain continuity in cloud-centric environments?

A. Ignoring Security Best Practices

B. Reducing Deployment Time

C. Identifying and Mitigating Risks Within the Supply Chain

D. Maximizing Costs

Answer: C - Identifying and Mitigating Risks Within the Supply Chain

Explanation: Organizations can maintain supply chain continuity by identifying and mitigating risks within the supply chain in cloud-centric environments.

Question 14:

How does business continuity planning extend beyond traditional disaster recovery efforts?

A. Ignoring Security Best Practices

B. Minimizing Costs

C. Ensuring Continuous Operation of Critical Functions

D. Maximizing Deployment Time

Answer: C - Ensuring Continuous Operation of Critical Functions

Explanation: Business continuity planning ensures the continuous operation of critical functions beyond traditional disaster recovery efforts.

Question 15:

What role do contingency plans play in business continuity?

A. Ignoring Security Best Practices

B. Reducing Deployment Time

C. Minimizing Disruptions by Providing Alternate Courses of Action

D. Maximizing Costs

Answer: C - Minimizing Disruptions by Providing Alternate Courses of Action

Explanation: Contingency plans minimize disruptions by providing alternate courses of action to maintain operations during unforeseen events.

Question 16:

Why is it important to regularly review and update business continuity plans?

A. Ignoring Security Best Practices

B. Reducing Deployment Time

C. Addressing Evolving Threats and Changes in the Environment

D. Maximizing Costs

Answer: C - Addressing Evolving Threats and Changes in the Environment

Explanation: Regular review and updates of business continuity plans are important to address evolving threats and changes in the environment, ensuring their effectiveness.

Question 17:

What are the benefits of having a dedicated business continuity team?

A. Ignoring Security Best Practices

B. Reducing Deployment Time

C. Ensuring a Coordinated Response and Accountability

D. Maximizing Costs

Answer: C - Ensuring a Coordinated Response and Accountability

Explanation: A dedicated business continuity team ensures a coordinated response and accountability during disruptions, minimizing the impact on operations.

Question 18:

How does business continuity planning contribute to organizational resilience?

A. Ignoring Security Best Practices

B. Reducing Deployment Time

C. Minimizing Downtime and Ensuring Rapid Recovery

D. Maximizing Costs

Answer: C - Minimizing Downtime and Ensuring Rapid Recovery

Explanation: Business continuity planning minimizes downtime and ensures rapid recovery, contributing to organizational resilience in the face of disruptions.

Question 19:

What measures can organizations take to enhance employee awareness of business continuity plans?

A. Ignoring Security Best Practices

B. Providing Regular Training and Education

C. Maximizing Costs

D. Reducing Deployment Time

Answer: B - Providing Regular Training and Education

Explanation: Providing regular training and education enhances employee awareness of business continuity plans, ensuring they are prepared to respond effectively during disruptions.

Question 20:

How can organizations ensure supply chain resilience in cloud-centric environments?

A. Ignoring Security Best Practices

B. Implementing Redundancy in Critical Supply Chain Components

C. Maximizing Costs

D. Reducing Deployment Time

Answer: B - Implementing Redundancy in Critical Supply Chain Components

Explanation: Organizations can ensure supply chain resilience by implementing redundancy in critical supply chain components in cloud-centric environments.

Question 21:

What role does performance monitoring play in cloud maintenance?

A. Ignoring Security Best Practices

B. Reducing Deployment Time

C. Identifying Bottlenecks and Optimizing Resource Utilization

D. Maximizing Costs

Answer: C - Identifying Bottlenecks and Optimizing Resource Utilization

Explanation: Performance monitoring helps identify bottlenecks and optimize resource utilization in cloud maintenance.

Question 22:

How can organizations ensure security updates are regularly applied in cloud maintenance?

A. Ignoring Security Best Practices

B. Establishing Patch Management Processes

C. Maximizing Costs

D. Reducing Deployment Time

Answer: B - Establishing Patch Management Processes

Explanation: Organizations can ensure security updates are regularly applied by establishing patch management processes in cloud maintenance.

Question 23:

What strategies can organizations implement to stay compliant with industry standards in cloud maintenance?

A. Ignoring Security Best Practices

B. Conducting Regular Audits and Assessments

C. Maximizing Costs

D. Reducing Deployment Time

Answer: B - Conducting Regular Audits and Assessments

Explanation: Organizations can stay compliant with industry standards by conducting regular audits and assessments in cloud maintenance.

Question 24:

How does cost management contribute to efficient cloud maintenance?

A. Ignoring Security Best Practices

B. Reducing Deployment Time

C. Maximizing Costs

D. Optimizing Resource Allocation and Controlling Expenditures

Answer: D - Optimizing Resource Allocation and Controlling Expenditures

Explanation: Cost management contributes to efficient cloud maintenance by optimizing resource allocation and controlling expenditures.

Question 25:

What are the benefits of implementing automated scaling strategies in cloud maintenance?

A. Ignoring Security Best Practices

B. Reducing Deployment Time

C. Ensuring Resources Match Demand and Minimizing Costs

D. Maximizing Costs

Answer: C - Ensuring Resources Match Demand and Minimizing Costs

Explanation: Automated scaling strategies ensure resources match demand and minimize costs in cloud maintenance by automatically adjusting resource allocation based on workload fluctuations.

Question 26:

Why is it important to monitor cloud performance in real-time?

A. Ignoring Security Best Practices

B. Reducing Deployment Time

C. Identifying Performance Issues and Proactively Addressing Them

D. Maximizing Costs

Answer: C - Identifying Performance Issues and Proactively Addressing Them

Explanation: Monitoring cloud performance in real-time helps identify performance issues and proactively address them to maintain optimal performance.

Question 27:

What measures can organizations take to optimize storage resources in cloud maintenance?

A. Ignoring Security Best Practices

B. Implementing Deduplication and Compression

C. Maximizing Costs

D. Reducing Deployment Time

Answer: B - Implementing Deduplication and Compression

Explanation: Organizations can optimize storage resources by implementing deduplication and compression techniques in cloud maintenance.

Question 28:

How does continuous monitoring contribute to security in cloud maintenance?

A. Ignoring Security Best Practices

B. Reducing Deployment Time

C. Detecting Anomalies and Responding to Security Threats in Real-Time

D. Maximizing Costs

Answer: C - Detecting Anomalies and Responding to Security Threats in Real-Time

Explanation: Continuous monitoring contributes to security in cloud maintenance by detecting anomalies and responding to security threats in real-time.

Question 29:

What role does regular data backup play in cloud maintenance?

A. Ignoring Security Best Practices

B. Reducing Deployment Time

C. Ensuring Data Availability and Minimizing Data Loss

D. Maximizing Costs

Answer: C - Ensuring Data Availability and Minimizing Data Loss

Explanation: Regular data backup ensures data availability and minimizes data loss in cloud maintenance by providing backup copies of critical data.

Question 30:

How can organizations ensure the reliability of cloud infrastructure in maintenance operations?

A. Ignoring Security Best Practices

B. Implementing Redundancy and Failover Mechanisms

C. Maximizing Costs

D. Reducing Deployment Time

Answer: B - Implementing Redundancy and Failover Mechanisms

Explanation: Organizations can ensure the reliability of cloud infrastructure by implementing redundancy and failover mechanisms in maintenance operations.

Chapter 7: Cloud Management

Cloud Metrics

Understanding Cloud Metrics:

Cloud metrics are essential for gaining insights into the performance and health of cloud environments. By understanding various cloud metrics, such as CPU utilization, network traffic, and storage usage, organizations can effectively monitor and manage their cloud resources. Monitoring and analyzing these metrics enable organizations to identify trends, detect anomalies, and optimize resource utilization to ensure optimal performance and cost efficiency. Key performance indicators (KPIs) aligned with business objectives provide valuable insights into the overall health and effectiveness of cloud deployments, guiding decision-making processes and strategic planning.

Delve into the various metrics used to measure the performance, availability, and efficiency of cloud resources. This includes metrics such as CPU utilization, network traffic, storage usage, and response times.

Monitoring and Analysis:

Learn how to effectively monitor and analyze cloud metrics to identify trends, anomalies, and areas for optimization. Discover tools and techniques for real-time monitoring and historical analysis to ensure optimal performance and resource utilization.

Key Performance Indicators (KPIs):

Identify key performance indicators relevant to cloud environments, such as uptime, response times, and cost per transaction. Understand how these KPIs align with business objectives and inform decision-making processes.

Adding and Removing Cloud Resources

Scalability and Elasticity:

Explore the concepts of scalability and elasticity in cloud computing, understanding how cloud resources can be dynamically scaled up or down based on demand. Learn best practices for designing scalable and elastic architectures to optimize resource utilization and cost efficiency.

Provisioning and Deprovisioning:

Gain insights into the process of provisioning and deprovisioning cloud resources. Understand the steps involved in provisioning new resources, as well as the importance of proper deprovisioning to avoid resource wastage and unnecessary costs.

Automation and Orchestration:

Discover the role of automation and orchestration in managing the lifecycle of cloud resources. Learn how automation tools and orchestration platforms can streamline the process of adding and removing resources, improving efficiency and reducing manual overhead.

The dynamic nature of cloud environments requires efficient processes for adding and removing resources to meet changing demand and optimize resource utilization. Scalability and elasticity enable organizations to scale resources up or down based on workload fluctuations, ensuring they have the right resources at the right time. Proper provisioning and deprovisioning of resources are crucial to avoid resource wastage and unnecessary costs. Automation and orchestration play a significant role in streamlining these processes, allowing organizations to automate repetitive tasks and orchestrate complex workflows for adding and removing cloud resources seamlessly.

By mastering cloud metrics and understanding the processes involved in adding and removing cloud resources, organizations can effectively manage their cloud

Practice Questions and Answers

Question 1:

What are some examples of cloud metrics used to measure performance and efficiency?

A. Network latency and storage capacity

B. Printer toner levels and office temperature

C. Employee productivity and customer satisfaction

D. Market share and revenue growth

Answer: A - Network latency and storage capacity

Explanation: Cloud metrics used to measure performance and efficiency include network latency, which measures the delay in data transmission, and storage capacity, which indicates the amount of data stored in the cloud.

Question 2:

Why is it important to monitor and analyze cloud metrics regularly?

A. To increase deployment time

B. To identify trends, anomalies, and areas for optimization

C. To reduce resource utilization

D. To ignore security best practices

Answer: B - To identify trends, anomalies, and areas for optimization

Explanation: Monitoring and analyzing cloud metrics regularly help identify trends, anomalies, and areas for optimization, enabling organizations to maintain optimal performance and resource utilization.

Question 3:

What are Key Performance Indicators (KPIs) in the context of cloud metrics?

A. Key attributes of cloud services

B. Physical hardware specifications

C. Performance benchmarks for cloud environments

D. Employee performance evaluations

Answer: C - Performance benchmarks for cloud environments

Explanation: KPIs in the context of cloud metrics are performance benchmarks used to measure the effectiveness and efficiency of cloud environments in meeting business objectives.

Question 4:

Which metric measures the amount of data transferred over a network in a given time period?

A. CPU utilization

B. Network traffic

C. Storage capacity

D. Response time

Answer: B - Network traffic

Explanation: Network traffic measures the amount of data transferred over a network in a given time period, indicating the level of network activity.

Question 5:

How can organizations use cloud metrics to optimize resource utilization?

A. By ignoring performance trends

B. By reducing deployment time

C. By analyzing resource usage patterns and adjusting configurations

D. By maximizing costs

Answer: C - By analyzing resource usage patterns and adjusting configurations

Explanation: Organizations can use cloud metrics to optimize resource utilization by analyzing resource usage patterns and adjusting configurations to match demand more efficiently.

Question 6:

What is the process of dynamically adjusting the number of cloud resources based on workload fluctuations called?

A. Scaling

B. Shrinking

C. Stagnating

D. Stopping

Answer: A - Scaling

Explanation: Scaling is the process of dynamically adjusting the number of cloud resources based on workload fluctuations to ensure optimal performance and resource utilization.

Question 7:

Why is proper provisioning and deprovisioning of cloud resources important?

A. To maximize costs

B. To minimize resource wastage and unnecessary costs

C. To increase deployment time

D. To ignore security best practices

Answer: B - To minimize resource wastage and unnecessary costs

Explanation: Proper provisioning and deprovisioning of cloud resources are important to minimize resource wastage and unnecessary costs, ensuring efficient resource utilization.

Question 8:

Which process involves allocating resources to meet demand in a cloud environment?

A. Provisioning

B. Deprovisioning

C. Scaling

D. Stopping

Answer: A - Provisioning

Explanation: Provisioning involves allocating resources to meet demand in a cloud environment, ensuring that sufficient resources are available to handle workload requirements.

Question 9:

What role do automation and orchestration play in managing cloud resources?

A. Increasing manual overhead

B. Ignoring performance trends

C. Streamlining the process of adding and removing resources

D. Reducing deployment time

Answer: C - Streamlining the process of adding and removing resources

Explanation: Automation and orchestration streamline the process of adding and removing resources by automating repetitive tasks and orchestrating complex workflows, reducing manual overhead and improving efficiency.

Question 10:

How do scalability and elasticity contribute to resource management in cloud environments?

A. By increasing manual intervention

B. By reducing resource utilization

C. By dynamically adjusting resource allocation based on demand

D. By maximizing costs

Answer: C - By dynamically adjusting resource allocation based on demand

Explanation: Scalability and elasticity contribute to resource management in cloud environments by dynamically adjusting resource allocation based on demand, ensuring optimal performance and resource utilization.

Question 11:

Which process involves removing unused or unnecessary cloud resources to optimize resource utilization?

A. Provisioning

B. Deprovisioning

C. Scaling

D. Stopping

Answer: B - Deprovisioning

Explanation: Deprovisioning involves removing unused or unnecessary cloud resources to optimize resource utilization and reduce costs.

Question 12:

What is the term for the process of automatically adjusting cloud resources based on predefined rules or policies?

A. Scaling

B. Provisioning

C. Automation

D. Orchestration

Answer: A - Scaling

Explanation: Scaling is the process of automatically adjusting cloud resources based on predefined rules or policies to ensure optimal performance and resource utilization.

Question 13:

How can organizations ensure efficient resource management in cloud environments?

A. By ignoring cloud metrics

B. By automating provisioning and deprovisioning processes

C. By increasing manual intervention

D. By maximizing resource wastage

Answer: B - By automating provisioning and deprovisioning processes

Explanation: Organizations can ensure efficient resource management in cloud environments by automating provisioning and deprovisioning processes, reducing manual intervention and optimizing resource utilization.

Question 14:

What role does orchestration play in managing cloud resources?

A. Increasing manual overhead

B. Streamlining complex workflows and coordinating resource provisioning

C. Ignoring performance trends

D. Reducing deployment time

Answer: B - Streamlining complex workflows and coordinating resource provisioning

Explanation: Orchestration plays a key role in managing cloud resources by streamlining complex workflows and coordinating resource provisioning, ensuring efficient resource management and optimization.

Question 15:

How do organizations benefit from automated scaling strategies in cloud environments?

A. By increasing manual intervention

B. By ignoring performance trends

C. By dynamically adjusting resource allocation based on demand

D. By maximizing resource wastage

Answer: C - By dynamically adjusting resource allocation based on demand

Explanation: Organizations benefit from automated scaling strategies in cloud environments by dynamically adjusting resource allocation based on demand, ensuring optimal performance and resource utilization.

Question 16:

Which metric measures the percentage of time a cloud service is available and accessible to users?

A. CPU utilization

B. Network latency

C. Uptime

D. Storage capacity

Answer: C - Uptime

Explanation: Uptime measures the percentage of time a cloud service is available and accessible to users, indicating its reliability and availability.

Question 17:

How can cloud metrics help organizations identify performance bottlenecks?

A. By increasing manual intervention

B. By ignoring performance trends

C. By analyzing metrics such as CPU utilization and response times

D. By maximizing costs

Answer: C - By analyzing metrics such as CPU utilization and response times

Explanation: Cloud metrics such as CPU utilization and response times can help organizations identify performance bottlenecks by highlighting areas where resources are underutilized or response times are high.

Question 18:

What is the purpose of setting performance thresholds in cloud monitoring?

A. To ignore cloud metrics

B. To increase manual intervention

C. To define acceptable performance levels and trigger alerts

D. To maximize costs

Answer: C - To define acceptable performance levels and trigger alerts

Explanation: Performance thresholds in cloud monitoring are set to define acceptable performance levels and trigger alerts when performance falls below these thresholds, enabling proactive intervention to address issues.

Question 19:

Which cloud metric measures the time it takes for a system to respond to a user's request?

A. Network latency

B. Storage capacity

C. Response time

D. Uptime

Answer: C - Response time

Explanation: Response time measures the time it takes for a system to respond to a user's request, indicating the system's responsiveness and performance.

Question 20:

How can organizations use cloud metrics to optimize cost management?

A. By ignoring performance trends

B. By analyzing resource utilization and identifying cost-saving opportunities

C. By increasing manual intervention

D. By maximizing resource wastage

Answer: B - By analyzing resource utilization and identifying cost-saving opportunities

Explanation: Organizations can use cloud metrics to optimize cost management by analyzing resource utilization and identifying cost-saving opportunities, such as rightsizing instances or leveraging reserved capacity.

Question 21:

What is the term for the process of adding additional cloud resources to handle increased workload demands?

A. Provisioning

B. Deprovisioning

C. Scaling out

D. Stopping

Answer: C - Scaling out

Explanation: Scaling out is the process of adding additional cloud resources to handle increased workload demands, ensuring that the system can accommodate growing traffic or processing requirements.

Question 22:

Why is it important to automate the provisioning and deprovisioning of cloud resources?

A. To increase manual intervention

B. To reduce human error and ensure consistency

C. To ignore performance trends

D. To maximize costs

Answer: B - To reduce human error and ensure consistency

Explanation: Automating the provisioning and deprovisioning of cloud resources helps reduce human error and ensure consistency in resource management processes, improving efficiency and reliability.

Question 23:

What role does elasticity play in cloud resource management?

A. By reducing resource utilization

B. By maximizing costs

C. By dynamically adjusting resource allocation based on demand

D. By increasing manual intervention

Answer: C - By dynamically adjusting resource allocation based on demand

Explanation: Elasticity in cloud resource management enables dynamic adjustment of resource allocation based on demand, ensuring that the system can scale resources up or down as needed to meet changing workload requirements.

Question 24:

How can organizations ensure efficient resource provisioning in cloud environments?

A. By ignoring cloud metrics

B. By automating provisioning processes and leveraging templates

C. By increasing manual intervention

D. By maximizing resource wastage

Answer: B - By automating provisioning processes and leveraging templates

Explanation: Organizations can ensure efficient resource provisioning in cloud environments by automating provisioning processes and leveraging templates to streamline resource allocation and deployment.

Question 25:

What is the term for the process of removing cloud resources that are no longer needed?

A. Provisioning

B. Deprovisioning

C. Scaling in

D. Starting

Answer: B - Deprovisioning

Explanation: Deprovisioning is the process of removing cloud resources that are no longer needed, helping organizations optimize resource utilization and reduce costs.

These additional practice questions further cover various aspects of cloud management, including cloud metrics, resource provisioning, deprovisioning, scalability, elasticity, and cost optimization. Each question is designed to test understanding and knowledge in these critical areas of cloud operations.

Question 26:

How can organizations use cloud metrics to improve capacity planning?

A. By ignoring performance trends

B. By analyzing historical data and forecasting future resource needs

C. By increasing manual intervention

D. By maximizing costs

Answer: B - By analyzing historical data and forecasting future resource needs

Explanation: Organizations can use cloud metrics to improve capacity planning by analyzing historical data and forecasting future resource needs, ensuring they have the necessary resources to meet demand.

Question 27:

What cloud metric measures the amount of processing capacity consumed by applications and services?

A. Network latency

B. CPU utilization

C. Response time

D. Uptime

Answer: B - CPU utilization

Explanation: CPU utilization measures the amount of processing capacity consumed by applications and services in a cloud environment, indicating the level of demand on computational resources.

Question 28:

Why is it important for organizations to establish baseline metrics in cloud monitoring?

A. To ignore performance trends

B. To increase manual intervention

C. To provide a reference point for evaluating changes in performance

D. To maximize costs

Answer: C - To provide a reference point for evaluating changes in performance

Explanation: Establishing baseline metrics in cloud monitoring provides a reference point for evaluating changes in performance over time, helping organizations identify deviations and potential issues.

Question 29:

How can organizations use cloud metrics to optimize resource allocation?

A. By ignoring cloud metrics

B. By randomly adjusting resource allocation

C. By analyzing resource usage patterns and adjusting allocations accordingly

D. By maximizing costs

Answer: C - By analyzing resource usage patterns and adjusting allocations accordingly

Explanation: Organizations can use cloud metrics to optimize resource allocation by analyzing resource usage patterns and adjusting allocations accordingly to ensure efficient utilization and performance.

Question 30:

What role does real-time monitoring play in cloud management?

A. Increasing manual intervention

B. Providing immediate insights into performance and health

C. Ignoring cloud metrics

D. Maximizing costs

Answer: B - Providing immediate insights into performance and health

Explanation: Real-time monitoring provides immediate insights into the performance and health of cloud environments, enabling organizations to respond quickly to issues and ensure optimal operation.

Chapter 8: Cloud Management Baselines, Performance, and SLAs

Measuring Your Deployment Against the Baseline

Understanding Baselines:

Explore the concept of baselines in cloud management, which serve as reference points for measuring performance, resource utilization, and other key metrics. Learn how to establish baselines by collecting historical data and analyzing trends over time.

Measuring Deployment Performance:

Discover techniques for measuring deployment performance against established baselines. This includes monitoring key performance indicators (KPIs), such as response times, uptime, and resource utilization, and comparing them to baseline values to identify deviations and areas for improvement.

Optimizing Deployment Efficiency:

Learn strategies for optimizing deployment efficiency based on baseline measurements. Explore methods for identifying bottlenecks, optimizing resource allocation, and fine-tuning configurations to maximize performance and cost-effectiveness.

Baselines are essential in cloud management as they provide a benchmark for measuring performance, resource utilization, and other key metrics. By establishing baselines through historical data collection and trend analysis, organizations can gain insights into typical behavior and set expectations for deployment performance.

Measuring deployment performance against baselines involves monitoring key performance indicators (KPIs) such as response times, uptime, and resource utilization. By comparing current metrics to baseline values, organizations can identify deviations and areas for improvement, enabling proactive intervention to address issues and optimize performance.

Optimizing deployment efficiency based on baseline measurements involves identifying bottlenecks, optimizing resource allocation, and fine-tuning configurations. By leveraging insights from baseline comparisons, organizations can make informed decisions to maximize performance and cost-effectiveness, ensuring their cloud deployments operate at peak efficiency.

This provides practical guidance on establishing baselines, measuring deployment performance, and optimizing efficiency to effectively manage cloud environments and meet performance objectives.

Practice Questions and Answers

What is the purpose of establishing baselines in cloud management?

A. To ignore performance trends

B. To provide a reference point for measuring performance and resource utilization

C. To increase manual intervention

D. To maximize costs

Answer: B - To provide a reference point for measuring performance and resource utilization

Explanation: Baselines serve as reference points for measuring performance and resource utilization in cloud management, helping organizations identify deviations and optimize efficiency.

Question 2:

How are baselines typically established in cloud management?

A. By randomly selecting values

B. By collecting historical data and analyzing trends over time

C. By ignoring cloud metrics

D. By maximizing costs

Answer: B - By collecting historical data and analyzing trends over time

Explanation: Baselines are typically established in cloud management by collecting historical data and analyzing trends over time to determine typical performance and resource utilization levels.

Question 3:

What key metrics are often used to measure deployment performance against baselines?

A. Employee productivity and customer satisfaction

B. Network latency and storage capacity

C. Response times, uptime, and resource utilization

D. Market share and revenue growth

Answer: C - Response times, uptime, and resource utilization

Explanation: Response times, uptime, and resource utilization are key metrics used to measure deployment performance against baselines in cloud management.

Question 4:

Why is it important to compare current performance metrics to established baselines?

A. To ignore performance trends

B. To increase manual intervention

C. To identify deviations and areas for improvement

D. To maximize costs

Answer: C - To identify deviations and areas for improvement

Explanation: Comparing current performance metrics to established baselines helps identify deviations and areas for improvement, enabling organizations to optimize deployment efficiency.

Question 5:

What actions can organizations take based on deviations from established baselines?

A. Ignore the deviations and continue as usual

B. Proactively intervene to address issues and optimize performance

C. Increase manual intervention

D. Maximize costs

Answer: B - Proactively intervene to address issues and optimize performance

Explanation: Organizations should proactively intervene to address issues and optimize performance when deviations from established baselines are identified, ensuring efficient cloud management.

Question 6:

How can organizations optimize deployment efficiency based on baseline measurements?

A. By ignoring cloud metrics

B. By randomly adjusting resource allocation

C. By identifying bottlenecks, optimizing resource allocation, and fine-tuning configurations

D. By maximizing costs

Answer: C - By identifying bottlenecks, optimizing resource allocation, and fine-tuning configurations

Explanation: Organizations can optimize deployment efficiency based on baseline measurements by identifying bottlenecks, optimizing resource allocation, and fine-tuning configurations to maximize performance and cost-effectiveness.

Question 7:

What role do key performance indicators (KPIs) play in measuring deployment performance against baselines?

A. They provide a reference point for measuring performance and resource utilization

B. They increase manual intervention

C. They maximize costs

D. They help organizations identify deviations and areas for improvement

Answer: D - They help organizations identify deviations and areas for improvement

Explanation: Key performance indicators (KPIs) help organizations identify deviations and areas for improvement when measuring deployment performance against baselines in cloud management.

Question 8:

How does analyzing trends over time contribute to establishing baselines in cloud management?

A. By randomly selecting values

B. By ignoring cloud metrics

C. By providing insights into typical performance and resource utilization levels

D. By maximizing costs

Answer: C - By providing insights into typical performance and resource utilization levels

Explanation: Analyzing trends over time provides insights into typical performance and resource utilization levels, contributing to the establishment of baselines in cloud management.

Question 9:

What is the primary benefit of comparing deployment performance to established baselines?

A. To increase manual intervention

B. To maximize costs

C. To identify deviations and areas for improvement

D. To ignore performance trends

Answer: C - To identify deviations and areas for improvement

Explanation: The primary benefit of comparing deployment performance to established baselines is to identify deviations and areas for improvement, enabling organizations to optimize efficiency.

Question 10:

How do baselines help organizations in cloud management?

A. By randomly adjusting resource allocation

B. By providing a reference point for measuring performance and resource utilization

C. By ignoring cloud metrics

D. By maximizing costs

Answer: B - By providing a reference point for measuring performance and resource utilization

Explanation: Baselines help organizations in cloud management by providing a reference point for measuring performance and resource utilization, enabling effective monitoring and optimization.

Question 11:

What is the significance of response times in measuring deployment performance against baselines?

A. Response times indicate the amount of data transferred over a network.

B. Response times provide insights into the reliability and availability of cloud services.

C. Response times measure the percentage of time a cloud service is available and accessible to users.

D. Response times measure the time it takes for a system to respond to a user's request.

Answer: D - Response times measure the time it takes for a system to respond to a user's request.

Explanation: Response times are crucial in measuring deployment performance against baselines as they directly reflect the system's responsiveness to user requests, helping identify potential bottlenecks or performance issues.

Question 12:

Why do organizations establish performance baselines in cloud management?

A. To randomly select values for resource utilization.

B. To provide historical data for comparison and analysis.

C. To increase manual intervention in deployment processes.

D. To maximize costs by ignoring performance trends.

Answer: B - To provide historical data for comparison and analysis.

Explanation: Organizations establish performance baselines in cloud management to provide historical data for comparison and analysis, enabling them to track performance trends and identify areas for improvement.

Question 13:

How does the comparison of current performance metrics to established baselines aid in optimization?

A. It enables organizations to ignore performance trends and continue as usual.

B. It provides insights into deviations and areas for improvement, allowing proactive intervention.

C. It increases manual intervention, complicating deployment processes.

D. It maximizes costs by disregarding efficiency metrics.

Answer: B - It provides insights into deviations and areas for improvement, allowing proactive intervention.

Explanation: Comparing current performance metrics to established baselines provides insights into deviations and areas for improvement, enabling organizations to proactively intervene and optimize deployment processes.

Question 14:

What is the primary purpose of analyzing trends over time in cloud management?

A. To randomly select values for resource allocation.

B. To provide historical data for comparison and analysis.

C. To increase manual intervention in deployment processes.

D. To maximize costs by ignoring performance trends.

Answer: B - To provide historical data for comparison and analysis.

Explanation: Analyzing trends over time in cloud management provides historical data for comparison and analysis, aiding in the establishment of baselines and identification of performance trends.

Question 15:

How do key performance indicators (KPIs) contribute to measuring deployment performance against baselines?

A. By providing a reference point for measuring performance and resource utilization.

B. By increasing manual intervention in deployment processes.

C. By ignoring cloud metrics and performance trends.

D. By maximizing costs through inefficient resource allocation.

Answer: A - By providing a reference point for measuring performance and resource utilization.

Explanation: Key performance indicators (KPIs) contribute to measuring deployment performance against baselines by providing a reference point for measuring performance and resource utilization, aiding in performance monitoring and optimization.

Question 16:

What action should organizations take when deviations from established baselines are identified?

A. Ignore the deviations and continue as usual.

B. Proactively intervene to address issues and optimize performance.

C. Increase manual intervention, complicating deployment processes.

D. Maximize costs by disregarding efficiency metrics.

Answer: B - Proactively intervene to address issues and optimize performance.

Explanation: When deviations from established baselines are identified, organizations should proactively intervene to address issues and optimize performance, ensuring efficient cloud management.

Question 17:

Why is it important for organizations to optimize deployment efficiency based on baseline measurements?

A. To randomly adjust resource allocation without considering performance metrics.

B. To provide historical data for comparison and analysis.

C. To increase manual intervention in deployment processes.

D. To maximize performance and cost-effectiveness.

Answer: D - To maximize performance and cost-effectiveness.

Explanation: Optimizing deployment efficiency based on baseline measurements is important for organizations to maximize performance and cost-effectiveness, ensuring efficient cloud management and resource utilization.

Question 18:

What is the role of baselines in cloud management?

A. To randomly select values for resource utilization.

B. To provide historical data for comparison and analysis.

C. To increase manual intervention in deployment processes.

D. To maximize costs by ignoring performance trends.

Answer: B - To provide historical data for comparison and analysis.

Explanation: The role of baselines in cloud management is to provide historical data for comparison and analysis, aiding in performance monitoring, optimization, and decision-making processes.

Question 19:

How do organizations benefit from comparing deployment performance to established baselines?

A. By ignoring performance trends and continuing as usual.

B. By proactively identifying deviations and areas for improvement.

C. By increasing manual intervention and complicating deployment processes.

D. By maximizing costs through inefficient resource allocation.

Answer: B - By proactively identifying deviations and areas for improvement.

Explanation: Organizations benefit from comparing deployment performance to established baselines by proactively identifying deviations and areas for improvement, enabling them to optimize performance and resource utilization.

Question 20:

What can organizations achieve by establishing baselines in cloud management?

A. To randomly adjust resource allocation without considering performance metrics.

B. To provide historical data for comparison and analysis.

C. To increase manual intervention in deployment processes.

D. To maximize costs by ignoring performance trends.

Answer: B - To provide historical data for comparison and analysis.

Explanation: By establishing baselines in cloud management, organizations can provide historical data for comparison and analysis, aiding in performance monitoring, optimization, and decision-making processes.

Question 21:

How can response times impact user experience in cloud deployments?

A. Response times are unrelated to user experience.

B. Longer response times may lead to slower application performance and decreased user satisfaction.

C. Response times have no effect on application performance.

D. Shorter response times increase the likelihood of errors and service interruptions.

Answer: B - Longer response times may lead to slower application performance and decreased user satisfaction.

Explanation: Response times directly impact user experience in cloud deployments. Longer response times can result in slower application performance, leading to decreased user satisfaction and potentially impacting business outcomes.

Question 22:

What advantage do historical data provide in establishing baselines for cloud management?

A. Historical data can be used to randomly select values for resource allocation.

B. Historical data increase manual intervention in deployment processes.

C. Historical data provide insights into typical performance and resource utilization levels.

D. Historical data maximize costs by ignoring performance trends.

Answer: C - Historical data provide insights into typical performance and resource utilization levels.

Explanation: Historical data offer insights into typical performance and resource utilization levels, aiding in the establishment of baselines for cloud management and facilitating performance monitoring and optimization.

Question 23:

In cloud management, why is it essential to track performance metrics against established baselines?

A. To ignore performance trends and continue as usual.

B. To increase manual intervention and complicating deployment processes.

C. To identify deviations and areas for improvement and optimize performance.

D. To maximize costs by disregarding efficiency metrics.

Answer: C - To identify deviations and areas for improvement and optimize performance.

Explanation: Tracking performance metrics against established baselines is crucial in cloud management to identify deviations and areas for improvement, enabling organizations to optimize performance and ensure efficient resource utilization.

Question 24:

What role do performance thresholds play in cloud management?

A. Performance thresholds are unrelated to cloud management.

B. Performance thresholds increase manual intervention in deployment processes.

C. Performance thresholds provide a reference point for acceptable performance levels and trigger alerts when exceeded.

D. Performance thresholds maximize costs by ignoring performance trends.

Answer: C - Performance thresholds provide a reference point for acceptable performance levels and trigger alerts when exceeded.

Explanation: Performance thresholds in cloud management provide a reference point for acceptable performance levels and trigger alerts when exceeded, enabling organizations to proactively address performance issues.

Question 25:

How do organizations benefit from analyzing trends over time in cloud management?

A. Analyzing trends over time increases manual intervention in deployment processes.

B. Analyzing trends over time provides historical data for comparison and analysis, aiding in performance monitoring and optimization.

C. Analyzing trends over time ignores performance trends and impacts user experience.

D. Analyzing trends over time maximizes costs by disregarding efficiency metrics.

Answer: B - Analyzing trends over time provides historical data for comparison and analysis, aiding in performance monitoring and optimization.

Explanation: Analyzing trends over time provides historical data for comparison and analysis, facilitating performance monitoring and optimization in cloud management.

Question 26:

What action should organizations take when performance metrics deviate significantly from established baselines?

A. Ignore the deviations and continue as usual.

B. Proactively intervene to address issues and optimize performance.

C. Increase manual intervention and complicating deployment processes.

D. Maximize costs by disregarding efficiency metrics.

Answer: B - Proactively intervene to address issues and optimize performance.

Explanation: When performance metrics deviate significantly from established baselines, organizations should proactively intervene to address issues and optimize performance, ensuring efficient cloud management.

Question 27:

How can organizations leverage baselines to optimize cloud resource allocation?

A. By randomly adjusting resource allocation without considering performance metrics.

B. By providing historical data for comparison and analysis, aiding in performance monitoring and optimization.

C. By increasing manual intervention and complicating deployment processes.

D. By maximizing costs through inefficient resource allocation.

Answer: B - By providing historical data for comparison and analysis, aiding in performance monitoring and optimization.

Explanation: Organizations can leverage baselines to optimize cloud resource allocation by providing historical data for comparison and analysis, aiding in performance monitoring and optimization.

Question 28:

What is the primary goal of optimizing deployment efficiency based on baseline measurements?

A. To randomly adjust resource allocation without considering performance metrics.

B. To increase manual intervention in deployment processes.

C. To maximize performance and cost-effectiveness.

D. To maximize costs by disregarding performance trends.

Answer: C - To maximize performance and cost-effectiveness.

Explanation: The primary goal of optimizing deployment efficiency based on baseline measurements is to maximize performance and cost-effectiveness, ensuring efficient cloud management and resource utilization.

Question 29:

Why do organizations use performance baselines in cloud management?

A. To randomly adjust resource allocation without considering performance metrics.

B. To provide historical data for comparison and analysis, aiding in performance monitoring and optimization.

C. To increase manual intervention and complicating deployment processes.

D. To maximize costs by ignoring performance trends.

Answer: B - To provide historical data for comparison and analysis, aiding in performance monitoring and optimization.

Explanation: Organizations use performance baselines in cloud management to provide historical data for comparison and analysis, facilitating performance monitoring, optimization, and decision-making processes.

Question 30:

What is the primary benefit of comparing deployment performance to established baselines?

A. To ignore performance trends and continue as usual.

B. To proactively identify deviations and areas for improvement.

C. To increase manual intervention and complicating deployment processes.

D. To maximize costs through inefficient resource allocation.

Answer: B - To proactively identify deviations and areas for improvement.

Explanation: The primary benefit of comparing deployment performance to established baselines is to proactively identify deviations and areas for improvement, enabling organizations to optimize performance and resource utilization.

Chapter 9: Troubleshooting

Incident Management

We will explore the essential aspects of incident management in cloud environments, focusing on identifying, prioritizing, and resolving incidents effectively.

Understanding Incident Management: Learn about the importance of incident management in maintaining the reliability and availability of cloud services. Explore the key components of an incident management process, including incident detection, logging, classification, prioritization, and resolution.

Incident Response Procedures: Discover best practices for developing incident response procedures tailored to cloud environments. Explore strategies for rapid incident detection, effective communication, escalation, and collaboration among stakeholders to minimize the impact of incidents.

Continuous Improvement: Learn how to leverage incident data and post-incident analysis to drive continuous improvement in incident management processes. Explore techniques for identifying root causes, implementing preventive measures, and enhancing incident response capabilities over time.

Troubleshooting Cloud Capacity Issues

Identifying Capacity Issues: Learn how to identify common signs of capacity issues in cloud environments, such as increased response times, resource exhaustion, and performance degradation. Explore techniques for monitoring and analyzing cloud resource utilization to detect capacity-related issues proactively.

Resolving Capacity Issues: Discover troubleshooting strategies for addressing cloud capacity issues effectively. Explore techniques for optimizing resource utilization, scaling resources dynamically, and implementing capacity planning practices to ensure adequate capacity and performance.

Troubleshooting Automation and Orchestration

Understanding Automation and Orchestration: Learn about the role of automation and orchestration in cloud environments and their impact on operational efficiency. Explore common challenges and pitfalls associated with automation and orchestration, such as script errors, integration issues, and workflow bottlenecks.

Troubleshooting Automation Failures: Discover troubleshooting techniques for diagnosing and resolving automation failures in cloud environments. Explore methods for debugging scripts, analyzing error logs, and verifying configuration settings to identify and rectify issues efficiently.

Optimizing Orchestration Workflows: Learn how to optimize orchestration workflows to improve performance, reliability, and maintainability. Explore strategies for streamlining workflow execution, optimizing resource allocation, and implementing error handling mechanisms to enhance automation efficiency.

By mastering the troubleshooting techniques covered in this chapter, cloud professionals can effectively address a wide range of issues encountered in cloud environments, ensuring optimal performance, reliability, and availability of cloud services.

Practice Questions and Answers

Question 1:

What is the primary goal of incident management in cloud environments?

A. To ignore incidents and continue operations as usual.

B. To identify, prioritize, and resolve incidents efficiently to minimize impact on services.

C. To increase the frequency of incidents to test system resilience.

D. To maximize costs by ignoring incident response procedures.

Answer: B - To identify, prioritize, and resolve incidents efficiently to minimize impact on services.

Explanation: The primary goal of incident management in cloud environments is to identify, prioritize, and resolve incidents efficiently to minimize their impact on services and ensure business continuity.

Question 2:

What are the key components of an incident management process?

A. Incident detection and resolution only.

B. Incident logging, classification, prioritization, and resolution.

C. Incident prioritization and resolution only.

D. Incident detection, escalation, and communication only.

Answer: B - Incident logging, classification, prioritization, and resolution.

Explanation: The key components of an incident management process include incident logging, classification, prioritization, and resolution, along with incident detection and escalation as necessary.

Question 3:

Why is it important to develop incident response procedures tailored to cloud environments?

A. To increase manual intervention and complicating incident resolution processes.

B. To ensure incidents are ignored and operations continue as usual.

C. To adapt incident response practices to the unique characteristics of cloud environments.

D. To maximize costs by disregarding incident response procedures.

Answer: C - To adapt incident response practices to the unique characteristics of cloud environments.

Explanation: Developing incident response procedures tailored to cloud environments is important to adapt incident response practices to the unique characteristics of cloud environments and ensure effective incident resolution.

Question 4:

What role does continuous improvement play in incident management?

A. Continuous improvement increases manual intervention and complicates incident resolution processes.

B. Continuous improvement ensures incidents are ignored and operations continue as usual.

C. Continuous improvement drives refinement and enhancement of incident management processes over time.

D. Continuous improvement maximizes costs by disregarding incident response procedures.

Answer: C - Continuous improvement drives refinement and enhancement of incident management processes over time.

Explanation: Continuous improvement in incident management drives refinement and enhancement of incident management processes over time, ensuring greater efficiency and effectiveness in incident response.

Question 5:

How can incident data and post-incident analysis contribute to continuous improvement in incident management?

A. Incident data and post-incident analysis increase manual intervention and complicating incident resolution processes.

B. Incident data and post-incident analysis ensure incidents are ignored and operations continue as usual.

C. Incident data and post-incident analysis provide insights into incident trends and root causes, informing preventive measures and process improvements.

D. Incident data and post-incident analysis maximize costs by disregarding incident response procedures.

Answer: C - Incident data and post-incident analysis provide insights into incident trends and root causes, informing preventive measures and process improvements.

Explanation: Incident data and post-incident analysis provide insights into incident trends and root causes, informing preventive measures and process improvements, thus contributing to continuous improvement in incident management.

Question 6:

What is the purpose of incident detection in cloud environments?

A. To maximize costs by disregarding incident response procedures.

B. To ignore incidents and continue operations as usual.

C. To identify and respond to incidents promptly to minimize their impact on services.

D. To increase the frequency of incidents to test system resilience.

Answer: C - To identify and respond to incidents promptly to minimize their impact on services.

Explanation: The purpose of incident detection in cloud environments is to identify and respond to incidents promptly to minimize their impact on services and ensure business continuity.

Question 7:

How does effective incident communication contribute to incident management?

A. Effective incident communication increases manual intervention and complicates incident resolution processes.

B. Effective incident communication ensures incidents are ignored and operations continue as usual.

C. Effective incident communication fosters collaboration and coordination among stakeholders, facilitating timely incident resolution.

D. Effective incident communication maximizes costs by disregarding incident response procedures.

Answer: C - Effective incident communication fosters collaboration and coordination among stakeholders, facilitating timely incident resolution.

Explanation: Effective incident communication fosters collaboration and coordination among stakeholders, facilitating timely incident resolution and minimizing the impact of incidents on services.

Question 8:

What is the purpose of incident classification in incident management?

A. To ignore incidents and continue operations as usual.

B. To maximize costs by disregarding incident response procedures.

C. To categorize incidents based on their impact and urgency to prioritize response efforts.

D. To increase the frequency of incidents to test system resilience.

Answer: C - To categorize incidents based on their impact and urgency to prioritize response efforts.

Explanation: The purpose of incident classification in incident management is to categorize incidents based on their impact and urgency to prioritize response efforts effectively.

Question 9:

Why is it important to prioritize incidents in incident management?

A. To maximize costs by disregarding incident response procedures.

B. To ignore incidents and continue operations as usual.

C. To focus response efforts on incidents with the greatest impact and urgency.

D. To increase the frequency of incidents to test system resilience.

Answer: C - To focus response efforts on incidents with the greatest impact and urgency.

Explanation: Prioritizing incidents in incident management ensures that response efforts are focused on incidents with the greatest impact and urgency, enabling efficient incident resolution and minimizing service disruptions.

Question 10:

What role does incident resolution play in incident management?

A. Incident resolution increases manual intervention and complicates incident resolution processes.

B. Incident resolution ensures incidents are ignored and operations continue as usual.

C. Incident resolution involves identifying and implementing solutions to address incidents effectively and restore normal operations.

D. Incident resolution maximizes costs by disregarding incident response procedures.

Answer: C - Incident resolution involves identifying and implementing solutions to address incidents effectively and restore normal operations.

Explanation: Incident resolution in incident management involves identifying and implementing solutions to address incidents effectively and restore normal operations, minimizing the impact of incidents on services.

Question 11:

What are common signs of cloud capacity issues?

A. Decreased response times and improved resource utilization.

B. Increased response times, resource exhaustion, and performance degradation.

C. Increased availability and scalability of cloud services.

D. Decreased resource utilization and uptime.

Answer: B - Increased response times, resource exhaustion, and performance degradation.

Explanation: Common signs of cloud capacity issues include increased response times, resource exhaustion (e.g., CPU, memory), and performance degradation due to insufficient resources to handle workload demands.

Question 12:

Why is it important to monitor cloud resource utilization for capacity management?

A. To ignore capacity issues and continue operations as usual.

B. To identify potential resource constraints and scalability challenges.

C. To decrease manual intervention in capacity management processes.

D. To maximize costs by disregarding capacity planning practices.

Answer: B - To identify potential resource constraints and scalability challenges.

Explanation: Monitoring cloud resource utilization is crucial for capacity management to identify potential resource constraints and scalability challenges, enabling proactive intervention to ensure optimal performance and availability.

Question 13:

What is the primary goal of troubleshooting cloud capacity issues?

A. To increase manual intervention and complicating capacity management processes.

B. To ignore capacity issues and continue operations as usual.

C. To identify and resolve resource constraints to optimize performance and scalability.

D. To maximize costs by disregarding capacity planning practices.

Answer: C - To identify and resolve resource constraints to optimize performance and scalability.

Explanation: The primary goal of troubleshooting cloud capacity issues is to identify and resolve resource constraints to optimize performance and scalability, ensuring the availability and reliability of cloud services.

Question 14:

How can organizations optimize cloud resource allocation to address capacity issues?

A. By randomly adjusting resource allocation without considering performance metrics.

B. By leveraging historical data and performance metrics to optimize resource allocation.

C. By increasing manual intervention and complicating capacity management processes.

D. By maximizing costs through inefficient resource allocation.

Answer: B - By leveraging historical data and performance metrics to optimize resource allocation.

Explanation: Organizations can optimize cloud resource allocation by leveraging historical data and performance metrics to inform resource allocation decisions, ensuring efficient utilization and performance.

Question 15:

What role does capacity planning play in troubleshooting cloud capacity issues?

A. Capacity planning increases manual intervention and complicates capacity management processes.

B. Capacity planning ensures incidents are ignored and operations continue as usual.

C. Capacity planning involves forecasting resource requirements and anticipating scalability needs to prevent capacity issues.

D. Capacity planning maximizes costs by disregarding capacity planning practices.

Answer: C - Capacity planning involves forecasting resource requirements and anticipating scalability needs to prevent capacity issues.

Explanation: Capacity planning involves forecasting resource requirements and anticipating scalability needs to prevent capacity issues, enabling proactive management of cloud capacity.

Question 16:

How can organizations dynamically scale resources to address capacity issues?

A. By randomly adjusting resource allocation without considering performance metrics.

B. By manually adjusting resource allocation based on workload demands.

C. By leveraging automation and orchestration tools to automatically adjust resource allocation based on workload fluctuations.

D. By maximizing costs through inefficient resource allocation.

Answer: C - By leveraging automation and orchestration tools to automatically adjust resource allocation based on workload fluctuations.

Explanation: Organizations can dynamically scale resources to address capacity issues by leveraging automation and orchestration tools to automatically adjust resource allocation based on workload fluctuations, ensuring optimal performance and scalability.

Question 17:

What is the purpose of capacity forecasting in cloud management?

A. To randomly adjust resource allocation without considering performance metrics.

B. To ignore capacity issues and continue operations as usual.

C. To anticipate future resource requirements and plan for scalability needs.

D. To maximize costs by disregarding capacity planning practices.

Answer: C - To anticipate future resource requirements and plan for scalability needs.

Explanation: The purpose of capacity forecasting in cloud management is to anticipate future resource requirements and plan for scalability needs, enabling proactive management of cloud capacity.

Question 18:

How do organizations benefit from proactive capacity management practices?

A. Proactive capacity management practices increase manual intervention and complicating capacity management processes.

B. Proactive capacity management practices ensure incidents are ignored and operations continue as usual.

C. Proactive capacity management practices enable organizations to prevent capacity issues and ensure optimal performance and scalability.

D. Proactive capacity management practices maximize costs by disregarding capacity planning practices.

Answer: C - Proactive capacity management practices enable organizations to prevent capacity issues and ensure optimal performance and scalability.

Explanation: Proactive capacity management practices enable organizations to prevent capacity issues and ensure optimal performance and scalability, minimizing the risk of service disruptions and downtime.

Question 19:

How can organizations optimize cloud capacity utilization to improve efficiency?

A. By randomly adjusting resource allocation without considering performance metrics.

B. By increasing manual intervention and complicating capacity management processes.

C. By analyzing resource utilization patterns and optimizing resource allocation based on workload demands.

D. By maximizing costs through inefficient resource allocation.

Answer: C - By analyzing resource utilization patterns and optimizing resource allocation based on workload demands.

Explanation: Organizations can optimize cloud capacity utilization by analyzing resource utilization patterns and optimizing resource allocation based on workload demands, ensuring efficient utilization and performance.

Question 20:

What role does scalability play in addressing cloud capacity issues?

A. Scalability increases manual intervention and complicates capacity management processes.

B. Scalability ensures incidents are ignored and operations continue as usual.

C. Scalability enables organizations to dynamically adjust resource allocation to meet changing workload demands.

D. Scalability maximizes costs by disregarding capacity planning practices.

Answer: C - Scalability enables organizations to dynamically adjust resource allocation to meet changing workload demands.

Explanation: Scalability enables organizations to dynamically adjust resource allocation to meet changing workload demands, ensuring optimal performance and availability in response to capacity fluctuations.

Question 21:

What is the role of automation and orchestration in cloud environments?

A. To manually execute tasks and processes without automation.

B. To streamline and automate the deployment, management, and scaling of cloud resources.

C. To increase manual intervention and complicating operational processes.

D. To ignore automation and orchestration tools and continue operations as usual.

Answer: B - To streamline and automate the deployment, management, and scaling of cloud resources.

Explanation: The role of automation and orchestration in cloud environments is to streamline and automate the deployment, management, and scaling of cloud resources, improving operational efficiency and consistency.

Question 22:

What are common challenges associated with automation and orchestration in cloud environments?

A. Increased efficiency and streamlined operations.

B. Integration issues, script errors, and workflow bottlenecks.

C. Decreased manual intervention and complexity in operational processes.

D. Ignoring automation and orchestration tools and continuing operations as usual.

Answer: B - Integration issues, script errors, and workflow bottlenecks.

Explanation: Common challenges associated with automation and orchestration in cloud environments include integration issues, script errors, and workflow bottlenecks, which can impact efficiency and effectiveness.

Question 23:

How can organizations troubleshoot automation failures in cloud environments?

A. By randomly executing automation scripts without analyzing errors.

B. By ignoring automation failures and continuing operations as usual.

C. By debugging scripts, analyzing error logs, and verifying configuration settings to identify and rectify issues.

D. By increasing manual intervention and complicating operational processes.

Answer: C - By debugging scripts, analyzing error logs, and verifying configuration settings to identify and rectify issues.

Explanation: Organizations can troubleshoot automation failures in cloud environments by debugging scripts, analyzing error logs, and verifying configuration settings to identify and rectify issues efficiently.

Question 24:

What is the purpose of optimizing orchestration workflows in cloud environments?

A. To manually execute tasks and processes without automation.

B. To streamline and optimize the execution of complex workflows and processes.

C. To increase manual intervention and complicating operational processes.

D. To ignore orchestration workflows and continue operations as usual.

Answer: B - To streamline and optimize the execution of complex workflows and processes.

Explanation: The purpose of optimizing orchestration workflows in cloud environments is to streamline and optimize the execution of complex workflows and processes, improving efficiency and reliability.

Question 25:

Why is it important to implement error handling mechanisms in orchestration workflows?

A. To manually execute tasks and processes without automation.

B. To ignore errors and continue operations as usual.

C. To minimize the impact of errors and failures on workflow execution and ensure reliability.

D. To increase manual intervention and complicating operational processes.

Answer: C - To minimize the impact of errors and failures on workflow execution and ensure reliability.

Explanation: It is important to implement error handling mechanisms in orchestration workflows to minimize the impact of errors and failures on workflow execution and ensure reliability and consistency.

Question 26:

How do organizations benefit from optimizing orchestration workflows?

A. By increasing manual intervention and complicating operational processes.

B. By streamlining and optimizing the execution of complex workflows and processes.

C. By ignoring errors and continuing operations as usual.

D. By manually executing tasks and processes without automation.

Answer: B - By streamlining and optimizing the execution of complex workflows and processes.

Explanation: Organizations benefit from optimizing orchestration workflows by streamlining and optimizing the execution of complex workflows and processes, improving efficiency and reliability.

Question 27:

What are common causes of automation and orchestration failures in cloud environments?

A. Increased efficiency and streamlined operations.

B. Script errors, integration issues, and misconfigured workflows.

C. Decreased manual intervention and complexity in operational processes.

D. Ignoring automation and orchestration tools and continuing operations as usual.

Answer: B - Script errors, integration issues, and misconfigured workflows.

Explanation: Common causes of automation and orchestration failures in cloud environments include script errors, integration issues, and misconfigured workflows, which can impact efficiency and effectiveness.

Question 28:

How can organizations optimize automation and orchestration processes to improve efficiency?

A. By randomly executing automation scripts without analyzing errors.

B. By increasing manual intervention and complicating operational processes.

C. By optimizing scripts, workflows, and integration points to streamline automation processes.

D. By ignoring errors and continuing operations as usual.

Answer: C - By optimizing scripts, workflows, and integration points to streamline automation processes.

Explanation: Organizations can optimize automation and orchestration processes by optimizing scripts, workflows, and integration points to streamline automation processes, improving efficiency and reliability.

Question 29:

What is the role of automation in incident response?

A. To increase manual intervention and complicating incident resolution processes.

B. To streamline and automate incident detection, analysis, and response processes.

C. To ignore incidents and continue operations as usual.

D. To manually execute incident response tasks without automation.

Answer: B - To streamline and automate incident detection, analysis, and response processes.

Explanation: The role of automation in incident response is to streamline and automate incident detection, analysis, and response processes, improving the efficiency and effectiveness of incident management.

Question 30:

How can organizations leverage orchestration tools to improve operational efficiency?

A. By manually executing tasks and processes without automation.

B. By increasing manual intervention and complicating operational processes.

C. By orchestrating the execution of workflows and processes to automate routine tasks and ensure consistency.

D. By ignoring orchestration tools and continuing operations as usual.

Answer: C - By orchestrating the execution of workflows and processes to automate routine tasks and ensure consistency.

Explanation: Organizations can leverage orchestration tools to improve operational efficiency by orchestrating the execution of workflows and processes to automate routine tasks and ensure consistency, reducing manual effort and errors.

Chapter 10: Troubleshooting Networking and Security Issues and Understanding Methodologies

Troubleshooting Cloud Networking Issues

We delve into the intricacies of troubleshooting networking issues in cloud environments, focusing on identifying, diagnosing, and resolving common networking challenges.

Understanding Cloud Networking: Gain insights into the fundamentals of cloud networking, including virtual networks, subnets, routing, and connectivity options. Explore the unique challenges and considerations involved in networking within cloud environments.

Identifying Networking Issues: Learn how to recognize signs of networking issues, such as latency, packet loss, connectivity issues, and DNS resolution problems. Discover effective monitoring and diagnostic tools for identifying and isolating networking problems.

Diagnosing and Resolving Issues: Explore troubleshooting techniques and best practices for diagnosing and resolving cloud networking issues efficiently. Learn how to analyze network traffic, review configuration settings, and implement corrective actions to restore network functionality.

Troubleshooting Security Issues

This focuses on troubleshooting security issues in cloud environments, addressing threats, vulnerabilities, and incidents that may compromise the security and integrity of cloud services.

Understanding Cloud Security: Explore the principles of cloud security, including data encryption, access control, identity management, and compliance requirements. Gain insights into the unique security challenges and considerations associated with cloud deployments.

Identifying Security Threats: Learn how to identify and classify security threats, such as malware, unauthorized access, data breaches, and insider threats. Discover proactive measures for detecting security incidents and anomalous activities in cloud environments.

Responding to Security Incidents: Discover effective incident response strategies and procedures for addressing security incidents in cloud environments. Explore techniques for containment, eradication, and recovery, as well as post-incident analysis and remediation efforts.

Troubleshooting Methodology

We discuss the overarching methodologies and approaches for troubleshooting issues in cloud environments, providing a structured framework for systematic problem-solving.

Understanding Troubleshooting Methodologies: Explore popular troubleshooting methodologies, such as the OSI model, TCP/IP model, and the troubleshooting process. Learn how to apply these methodologies to effectively diagnose and resolve issues in cloud deployments.

Practical Troubleshooting Techniques: Gain practical insights into troubleshooting techniques, including divide and conquer, bottom-up analysis, and hypothesis testing. Discover how to systematically isolate and address issues at different layers of the cloud infrastructure stack.

Continuous Improvement: Learn how to leverage incident data, post-mortem analysis, and feedback loops to drive continuous improvement in troubleshooting processes. Explore strategies for documenting lessons learned, updating documentation, and refining troubleshooting procedures over time.

By mastering the troubleshooting methodologies and techniques covered in this chapter, cloud professionals can effectively address networking and security issues, ensuring the reliability, availability, and security of cloud services.

Practice Questions and Answers

Question 1:

What are some common signs of networking issues in cloud environments?

A. Increased data encryption and access control measures.

B. Latency, packet loss, connectivity issues, and DNS resolution problems.

C. Decreased network traffic and improved performance.

D. Enhanced routing and subnets configuration.

Answer: B - Latency, packet loss, connectivity issues, and DNS resolution problems.

Explanation: Common signs of networking issues in cloud environments include latency, packet loss, connectivity issues (e.g., dropped connections), and DNS resolution problems.

Question 2:

What is the first step in troubleshooting cloud networking issues?

A. Implementing additional security measures.

B. Analyzing network traffic using diagnostic tools.

C. Checking network configuration settings and connectivity.

D. Ignoring networking issues and continuing operations as usual.

Answer: C - Checking network configuration settings and connectivity.

Explanation: The first step in troubleshooting cloud networking issues is to check network configuration settings and connectivity to identify any misconfigurations or connectivity problems.

Question 3:

How can organizations diagnose network latency issues in cloud environments?

A. By increasing network bandwidth allocation.

B. By analyzing network traffic patterns and identifying bottlenecks.

C. By implementing additional security measures.

D. By ignoring latency issues and continuing operations as usual.

Answer: B - By analyzing network traffic patterns and identifying bottlenecks.

Explanation: Organizations can diagnose network latency issues in cloud environments by analyzing network traffic patterns and identifying bottlenecks that may be causing delays.

Question 4:

What role do diagnostic tools play in troubleshooting cloud networking issues?

A. Diagnostic tools increase manual intervention and complicating troubleshooting processes.

B. Diagnostic tools ensure networking issues are ignored and operations continue as usual.

C. Diagnostic tools help analyze network traffic, identify problems, and troubleshoot issues efficiently.

D. Diagnostic tools maximize costs by disregarding troubleshooting efforts.

Answer: C - Diagnostic tools help analyze network traffic, identify problems, and troubleshoot issues efficiently.

Explanation: Diagnostic tools play a crucial role in troubleshooting cloud networking issues by helping analyze network traffic, identify problems, and troubleshoot issues efficiently.

Question 5:

What is the purpose of analyzing network traffic when troubleshooting cloud networking issues?

A. To increase manual intervention and complicating troubleshooting processes.

B. To ensure networking issues are ignored and operations continue as usual.

C. To identify patterns, anomalies, and potential causes of networking problems.

D. To maximize costs by disregarding troubleshooting efforts.

Answer: C - To identify patterns, anomalies, and potential causes of networking problems.

Explanation: Analyzing network traffic when troubleshooting cloud networking issues helps identify patterns, anomalies, and potential causes of networking problems, facilitating efficient troubleshooting and resolution.

Question 6:

How can organizations diagnose connectivity issues in cloud environments?

A. By ignoring connectivity issues and continuing operations as usual.

B. By analyzing network traffic patterns and identifying bottlenecks.

C. By checking network configuration settings and verifying connectivity between network components.

D. By implementing additional security measures.

Answer: C - By checking network configuration settings and verifying connectivity between network components.

Explanation: Organizations can diagnose connectivity issues in cloud environments by checking network configuration settings and verifying connectivity between network components to identify any misconfigurations or connectivity problems.

Question 7:

What troubleshooting approach is recommended for resolving cloud networking issues?

A. Dividing the problem into smaller parts and addressing each part individually.

B. Ignoring networking issues and continuing operations as usual.

C. Increasing manual intervention and complicating troubleshooting processes.

D. Implementing additional security measures.

Answer: A - Dividing the problem into smaller parts and addressing each part individually.

Explanation: The recommended troubleshooting approach for resolving cloud networking issues is to divide the problem into smaller parts and address each part individually, facilitating systematic problem-solving and resolution.

Question 8:

How can organizations troubleshoot DNS resolution problems in cloud environments?

A. By analyzing network traffic patterns and identifying bottlenecks.

B. By implementing additional security measures.

C. By checking DNS configuration settings and verifying DNS resolution processes.

D. By ignoring DNS resolution problems and continuing operations as usual.

Answer: C - By checking DNS configuration settings and verifying DNS resolution processes.

Explanation: Organizations can troubleshoot DNS resolution problems in cloud environments by checking DNS configuration settings and verifying DNS resolution processes to identify and rectify any misconfigurations or issues.

Question 9:

What role does network configuration play in troubleshooting cloud networking issues?

A. Network configuration increases manual intervention and complicates troubleshooting processes.

B. Network configuration ensures networking issues are ignored and operations continue as usual.

C. Network configuration settings may introduce misconfigurations or errors that contribute to networking problems.

D. Network configuration maximizes costs by disregarding troubleshooting efforts.

Answer: C - Network configuration settings may introduce misconfigurations or errors that contribute to networking problems.

Explanation: Network configuration settings may introduce misconfigurations or errors that contribute to networking problems, underscoring the importance of checking and verifying network configuration when troubleshooting cloud networking issues.

Question 10:

What are some best practices for resolving cloud networking issues efficiently?

A. Ignoring networking issues and continuing operations as usual.

B. Analyzing network traffic patterns and identifying bottlenecks.

C. Checking network configuration settings, using diagnostic tools, and following a systematic troubleshooting approach.

D. Implementing additional security measures.

Answer: C - Checking network configuration settings, using diagnostic tools, and following a systematic troubleshooting approach.

Explanation: Best practices for resolving cloud networking issues efficiently include checking network configuration settings, using diagnostic tools to analyze network traffic, and following a systematic troubleshooting approach to identify and address problems effectively.

Question 11:

What are some common security threats in cloud environments?

A. Increased data encryption and access control measures.

B. Malware, unauthorized access, data breaches, and insider threats.

C. Decreased security measures and enhanced accessibility.

D. Improved security posture and reduced vulnerability.

Answer: B - Malware, unauthorized access, data breaches, and insider threats.

Explanation: Common security threats in cloud environments include malware, unauthorized access, data breaches (e.g., loss or theft of sensitive data), and insider threats.

Question 12:

What is the first step in responding to a security incident in a cloud environment?

A. Ignoring the incident and continuing operations as usual.

B. Containment, isolating affected systems or resources to prevent further damage.

C. Conducting a post-incident analysis to identify the root cause of the incident.

D. Implementing additional security measures.

Answer: B - Containment, isolating affected systems or resources to prevent further damage.

Explanation: The first step in responding to a security incident in a cloud environment is containment, which involves isolating affected systems or resources to prevent further damage or spread of the incident.

Question 13:

How can organizations detect anomalous activities and potential security threats in cloud environments?

A. By decreasing security measures and enhancing accessibility.

B. By implementing additional security measures.

C. By analyzing security logs, monitoring network traffic, and using intrusion detection systems (IDS) or intrusion prevention systems (IPS).

D. By ignoring security threats and continuing operations as usual.

Answer: C - By analyzing security logs, monitoring network traffic, and using intrusion detection systems (IDS) or intrusion prevention systems (IPS).

Explanation: Organizations can detect anomalous activities and potential security threats in cloud environments by analyzing security logs, monitoring network traffic, and using intrusion detection systems (IDS) or intrusion prevention systems (IPS) to identify suspicious behavior or indicators of compromise.

Question 14:

What role does access control play in mitigating security risks in cloud environments?

A. Access control increases security risks by providing unauthorized access to resources.

B. Access control ensures incidents are ignored and operations continue as usual.

C. Access control limits access to resources based on predefined policies and permissions, reducing the risk of unauthorized access and data breaches.

D. Access control maximizes costs by disregarding security measures.

Answer: C - Access control limits access to resources based on predefined policies and permissions, reducing the risk of unauthorized access and data breaches.

Explanation: Access control limits access to resources based on predefined policies and permissions, reducing the risk of unauthorized access and data breaches in cloud environments.

Question 15:

What is the purpose of conducting a post-incident analysis in cloud security?

A. To ignore security incidents and continue operations as usual.

B. To decrease security measures and enhance accessibility.

C. To identify the root cause of security incidents, lessons learned, and areas for improvement.

D. To implement additional security measures.

Answer: C - To identify the root cause of security incidents, lessons learned, and areas for improvement.

Explanation: The purpose of conducting a post-incident analysis in cloud security is to identify the root cause of security incidents, gather lessons learned, and identify areas for improvement to prevent similar incidents in the future.

Question 16:

What is the role of encryption in cloud security?

A. Encryption increases security risks by providing unauthorized access to encrypted data.

B. Encryption ensures incidents are ignored and operations continue as usual.

C. Encryption protects sensitive data by converting it into a coded format that can only be accessed by authorized parties with the corresponding decryption keys.

D. Encryption maximizes costs by disregarding security measures.

Answer: C - Encryption protects sensitive data by converting it into a coded format that can only be accessed by authorized parties with the corresponding decryption keys.

Explanation: Encryption protects sensitive data in cloud environments by converting it into a coded format that can only be accessed by authorized parties with the corresponding decryption keys, enhancing security and confidentiality.

Question 17:

How can organizations prevent unauthorized access in cloud environments?

A. By ignoring security measures and continuing operations as usual.

B. By implementing additional security measures.

C. By enforcing strong authentication mechanisms, access controls, and identity management practices.

D. By decreasing security measures and enhancing accessibility.

Answer: C - By enforcing strong authentication mechanisms, access controls, and identity management practices.

Explanation: Organizations can prevent unauthorized access in cloud environments by enforcing strong authentication mechanisms, access controls, and identity management practices to ensure that only authorized users have access to resources.

Question 18:

What is the purpose of implementing intrusion detection systems (IDS) and intrusion prevention systems (IPS) in cloud environments?

A. To ignore security incidents and continue operations as usual.

B. To decrease security measures and enhance accessibility.

C. To detect and respond to suspicious activities and security threats in real-time.

D. To implement additional security measures.

Answer: C - To detect and respond to suspicious activities and security threats in real-time.

Explanation: The purpose of implementing intrusion detection systems (IDS) and intrusion prevention systems (IPS) in cloud environments is to detect and respond to suspicious activities and security threats in real-time, enhancing security posture and resilience.

Question 19:

How can organizations ensure compliance with security regulations and standards in cloud environments?

A. By ignoring security regulations and standards.

B. By implementing additional security measures.

C. By conducting regular audits, assessments, and reviews to ensure adherence to security regulations and standards.

D. By decreasing security measures and enhancing accessibility.

Answer: C - By conducting regular audits, assessments, and reviews to ensure adherence to security regulations and standards.

Explanation: Organizations can ensure compliance with security regulations and standards in cloud environments by conducting regular audits, assessments, and reviews to ensure adherence to relevant security requirements and guidelines.

Question 20:

What are some best practices for maintaining security in cloud environments?

A. Ignoring security measures and continuing operations as usual.

B. Implementing additional security measures.

C. Enforcing strong authentication, access controls, encryption, regular security audits, and employee training on security best practices.

D. Decreasing security measures and enhancing accessibility.

Answer: C - Enforcing strong authentication, access controls, encryption, regular security audits, and employee training on security best practices.

Explanation: Best practices for maintaining security in cloud environments include enforcing strong authentication, access controls, encryption, conducting regular security audits, and providing employee training on security best practices to mitigate risks and enhance security posture.

Question 21:

What is the purpose of following a structured troubleshooting methodology?

A. To increase manual intervention and complicating troubleshooting processes.

B. To ensure incidents are ignored and operations continue as usual.

C. To provide a systematic approach for identifying, diagnosing, and resolving issues efficiently.

D. To implement additional security measures.

Answer: C - To provide a systematic approach for identifying, diagnosing, and resolving issues efficiently.

Explanation: The purpose of following a structured troubleshooting methodology is to provide a systematic approach for identifying, diagnosing, and resolving issues efficiently, enhancing the effectiveness and reliability of troubleshooting efforts.

Question 22:

What role does documentation play in troubleshooting methodology?

A. Documentation increases manual intervention and complicating troubleshooting processes.

B. Documentation ensures incidents are ignored and operations continue as usual.

C. Documentation provides a record of troubleshooting steps, findings, and resolutions, facilitating knowledge sharing and future reference.

D. Documentation maximizes costs by disregarding troubleshooting efforts.

Answer: C - Documentation provides a record of troubleshooting steps, findings, and resolutions, facilitating knowledge sharing and future reference.

Explanation: Documentation provides a record of troubleshooting steps, findings, and resolutions, facilitating knowledge sharing and future reference, improving collaboration and efficiency.

Question 23:

What is the significance of defining a scope when troubleshooting issues?

A. To increase manual intervention and complicating troubleshooting processes.

B. To ensure incidents are ignored and operations continue as usual.

C. To clearly define the boundaries and objectives of the troubleshooting effort, focusing efforts on specific areas or components.

D. To implement additional security measures.

Answer: C - To clearly define the boundaries and objectives of the troubleshooting effort, focusing efforts on specific areas or components.

Explanation: Defining a scope when troubleshooting issues helps to clearly define the boundaries and objectives of the troubleshooting effort, focusing efforts on specific areas or components and avoiding unnecessary distractions or deviations.

Question 24:

What is the role of hypothesis testing in troubleshooting methodology?

A. To increase manual intervention and complicating troubleshooting processes.

B. To ensure incidents are ignored and operations continue as usual.

C. To formulate and test hypotheses or theories about the root cause of the issue, guiding the troubleshooting process.

D. To implement additional security measures.

Answer: C - To formulate and test hypotheses or theories about the root cause of the issue, guiding the troubleshooting process.

Explanation: Hypothesis testing in troubleshooting methodology involves formulating and testing hypotheses or theories about the root cause of the issue, guiding the troubleshooting process and helping to identify potential solutions.

Question 25:

What is the purpose of following a step-by-step troubleshooting process?

A. To increase manual intervention and complicating troubleshooting processes.

B. To ensure incidents are ignored and operations continue as usual.

C. To provide a structured approach for systematically identifying, isolating, and resolving issues, reducing the risk of overlooking critical steps or causing further disruptions.

D. To implement additional security measures.

Answer: C - To provide a structured approach for systematically identifying, isolating, and resolving issues, reducing the risk of overlooking critical steps or causing further disruptions.

Explanation: Following a step-by-step troubleshooting process provides a structured approach for systematically identifying, isolating, and resolving issues, reducing the risk of overlooking critical steps or causing further disruptions during the troubleshooting process.

Question 26:

What is the role of collaboration in troubleshooting methodology?

A. To increase manual intervention and complicating troubleshooting processes.

B. To ensure incidents are ignored and operations continue as usual.

C. To facilitate communication, knowledge sharing, and collective problem-solving efforts among team members or stakeholders involved in the troubleshooting process.

D. To implement additional security measures.

Answer: C - To facilitate communication, knowledge sharing, and collective problem-solving efforts among team members or stakeholders involved in the troubleshooting process.

Explanation: Collaboration in troubleshooting methodology facilitates communication, knowledge sharing, and collective problem-solving efforts among team members or stakeholders involved in the troubleshooting process, improving efficiency and effectiveness.

Question 27:

Why is it important to verify the solution after troubleshooting an issue?

A. To increase manual intervention and complicating troubleshooting processes.

B. To ensure incidents are ignored and operations continue as usual.

C. To confirm that the issue has been successfully resolved and validate the effectiveness of the solution implementation.

D. To implement additional security measures.

Answer: C - To confirm that the issue has been successfully resolved and validate the effectiveness of the solution implementation.

Explanation: Verifying the solution after troubleshooting an issue is important to confirm that the issue has been successfully resolved and validate the effectiveness of the solution implementation, ensuring that the problem does not recur.

Question 28:

What is the significance of conducting a lessons learned session after troubleshooting an issue?

A. To increase manual intervention and complicating troubleshooting processes.

B. To ensure incidents are ignored and operations continue as usual.

C. To reflect on the troubleshooting process, identify successes and challenges, and capture insights and recommendations for future improvements.

D. To implement additional security measures.

Answer: C - To reflect on the troubleshooting process, identify successes and challenges, and capture insights and recommendations for future improvements.

Explanation: Conducting a lessons learned session after troubleshooting an issue allows teams to reflect on the troubleshooting process, identify successes and challenges, and capture insights and recommendations for future improvements, promoting continuous learning and improvement.

Question 29:

What are some common troubleshooting methodologies used in IT?

A. Ignoring troubleshooting methodologies and continuing operations as usual.

B. OSI model, TCP/IP model, and divide and conquer approach.

C. Increasing manual intervention and complicating troubleshooting processes.

D. Implementing additional security measures.

Answer: B - OSI model, TCP/IP model, and divide and conquer approach.

Explanation: Common troubleshooting methodologies used in IT include the OSI model, TCP/IP model, and divide and conquer approach, providing structured frameworks for systematically identifying, isolating, and resolving issues.

Question 30:

How can organizations improve their troubleshooting processes over time?

A. By ignoring troubleshooting efforts and continuing operations as usual.

B. By implementing additional security measures.

C. By leveraging incident data, conducting post-mortem analysis, and incorporating feedback to refine troubleshooting procedures and enhance effectiveness.

D. By increasing manual intervention and complicating troubleshooting processes.

Answer: C - By leveraging incident data, conducting post-mortem analysis, and incorporating feedback to refine troubleshooting procedures and enhance effectiveness.

Explanation: Organizations can improve their troubleshooting processes over time by leveraging incident data, conducting post-mortem analysis, and incorporating feedback from stakeholders to refine troubleshooting procedures and enhance effectiveness, promoting continuous improvement and resilience.

Conclusion

In the dynamic landscape of cloud computing, the ability to troubleshoot effectively is paramount for maintaining the reliability, security, and performance of cloud environments. Throughout this book, we have explored the essential principles, methodologies, and best practices for troubleshooting various aspects of cloud computing configurations, deployments, security, and operations.

From identifying and diagnosing networking issues to mitigating security threats and implementing disaster recovery plans, each chapter has provided valuable insights and practical guidance for addressing common challenges encountered in cloud environments. By following structured troubleshooting methodologies, leveraging diagnostic tools, and fostering collaboration among team members, organizations can streamline the troubleshooting process and minimize downtime.

Moreover, the importance of continuous improvement cannot be overstated. By conducting post-mortem analyses, documenting lessons learned, and incorporating feedback loops, organizations can refine their troubleshooting processes and enhance their resilience to future challenges. Additionally, staying abreast of emerging technologies, security trends, and best practices is crucial for staying ahead of potential issues and maintaining a proactive approach to troubleshooting.

As cloud computing continues to evolve, the skills and knowledge gained from mastering troubleshooting techniques will remain invaluable for IT professionals and organizations alike. By embracing a proactive mindset, cultivating a culture of collaboration, and continuously refining their troubleshooting processes, organizations can navigate the complexities of cloud computing with confidence, ensuring the continued success of their cloud initiatives.

I hope that this book has served as a comprehensive guide and valuable resource for individuals and organizations seeking to enhance their troubleshooting capabilities in the ever-changing landscape of cloud computing. May the principles and practices outlined within these pages empower you to tackle any challenge that arises and unlock the full potential of cloud technology.